Unlocking

the

Doors

Unlocking the Doors

A Woman's Struggle Against Intolerance

Eva Olsson

Copyright © by Eva Olsson 2001

Cover Design: Cynthia Koelsch

Cover Artwork: Laura Thompson

Cover Photographs: Ron Jacques

Printed in Canada

ISBN 1-890412-50-3

Libray of Congress Cataloging

10 9   8   7   6   5   4   3   2

Published by Eva Olsson

Bracebridge, Ontario

This book is dedicated to my son, Jan,

my grandchildren Brenna, Rudy,

and Alexandra Leah,

and all those who did not survive

to speak for themselves.

Acknowledgements

George Boreland, Joel Dart, and Eleanor Flynn for their help, especially with the early transcriptions of my tapes.

The editor and staff of the Orillia Packet and Times for their support.

Jennifer Garrow Sneyd, Cheryl Goldthorp and my lawyer, Dan Wyjad, for their ongoing assistance.

Jackie Doran for over forty years of friendship and for her encouragement and support for this project.

Bonnie Dart, Renee Smith, and Martha Scott for their continued support and for believing in my project.

Ron Jacques, my editor, who arrives by canoe for our meetings. Without him this book wouldn't be where it is today. The time required to turn my story from transcriptions of tapes into a book was so generously given to me. I will forever be grateful for his caring support.

Contents

Introduction

Chapter 1   Early Childhood   1

Chapter 2   Home Life   15

Chapter 3   Adolescence and Rebellion   19

Chapter 4   Mama   33

Chapter 5   Sarah's Wedding   39

Chapter 6   German Occupation   45

Chapter 7   Auschwitz   51

Chapter 8   Slave Labour   59

Chapter 9   Bergen-Belsen   73

Chapter 10   Liberation   83

Chapter 11   Sweden   91

Chapter 12   Rude   97

Chapter 13   Canada   111

Chapter 14   Rude's Accident   123

Chapter 15   Fradel   129

Chapter 16   Being Different   139

Chapter 17   Denial   143

Chapter 18   Freedom   153

Contents

Chapter 19   Religion   157

Chapter 20   Teaching Children   163

Chapter 21   The Danes   171

Chapter 22   Jackie   175

Chapter 23   Working   181

Chapter 24   My Grandchildren   185

Chapter 25   Speaking To Students   195

Epilogue   201

FOREWORD

Dear Eva,

It is the day following your visit to my World Issues class. My students are writing you letters right now, so it is also an opportunity for me to put my thoughts about you to paper. In the early hours of the morning I awoke with thoughts of you floating through my head and heart. I realized that your many visits to my classrooms over the past couple of years have drawn our spirits closer together. Yesterday when you talked about your final moments with your mother, I felt that I was there with you at the camp, feeling your pain, supporting you and comforting you in spirit. I felt this spiritual bond very strongly as I awoke this morning. It was a lovely healing strength mixed with sadness and joy — sadness for your life's unforgivable tragedies, and joy that a loving God is healing you through the human spirit. It is totally clear to me now why you have not lost faith in humanity. God enables our spirits to transcend the physical limitations of this world. The profound horrors and fears you have survived attest to that fact.

Your message is getting stronger and more and more powerful. I feel it is so because you are being strengthened through the process of inspiring young people with your sacred message of tolerance, a most important mission.

When you share your story I am so thankful

for your tears and smiles and laughter. Each time my students and I cry and smile with you, we do so for the millions of others who are no longer able to cry and smile. Our human spirit must bridge the dark pit of ignorance to bring light and awareness to the racism in our world. Your message is strong and secure in the hearts and minds of hundreds of young people you have spoken to. You are living history that demands their attention and most importantly, their action to fight racism wherever they encounter it.

Each time I see you and we embrace I feel the warmth of your spirit. It is very evident to me why you are a survivor. Thank you for sharing your intimate experiences with me.

Love,

Bonnie
(Bonnie Dart, Bracebridge & Muskoka Lakes Secondary School)

Introduction

I am a survivor. My struggle to survive began even before I was born. Mama told me that she was unwell when she was pregnant with me and the doctor told her she should have an abortion. My father did not agree with the doctor and went to see the head rabbi who told my father that an abortion was not necessary. Mama was put on a strict diet and stayed in bed for the whole pregnancy.

I was born into a tightly controlled Hasidic environment, where my parents, following their religious beliefs, denied me an education and prevented me from learning about the world through contact with people, books and movies. My spiritual yearnings and curiosity about the world around me were ignored at first, then repressed and punished. When I was in my teens World War II started and the Nazis did everything they could during the Holocaust to deny me my dignity as a human being. In the end they failed but for 50 years I was unable to speak about that period of pain and suffering. On many occasions I considered writing down the story of my experiences at home as a child and in two concentration camps, Auschwitz and Bergen-Belsen, but I was unable to release these memories. Having grandchildren gave me the strength and resolve to begin my mission to speak out about what I endured and witnessed. I realize how important it is for them and for future generations to have this information.

If I can help anyone to understand where racism and intolerance lead, then my mission is being fulfilled. Although putting it on paper is a difficult task, I have made a commitment to others and myself and I must put my personal pain aside. I cannot live in the past but I must live with it. Perhaps writing my story will weaken the hold the past has had on me.

In 1996, when I was 72, my granddaughter Brenna interviewed me for a school project. When her teacher read her paper she invited me to come and speak to her classes about the Holocaust. The talk went well and the student responses were very positive, so I was asked to return and speak again. These two episodes made me realize the importance of sharing my story with the next generation. I decided that my mission in life would be to speak about the Holocaust for those victims who cannot speak for themselves, and to help make sure such an event never happens again — to anyone.

I have received over a thousand letters so far from elementary and high school students, and they sure let me know how they feel. Their letters give me the courage to carry on, knowing that I am no longer alone. On days when my spirits are a little low, I read those letters and take hope from what they say. Their responses indicate the importance of my visits to their classes and their need to know what happened to six million Jews and five million non-Jews — Gypsies, homosexuals, disabled people, political activists, and others —at the hands of the Nazis and their supporters in many countries during World War

II. The following letter and essay show me that my message is being understood:

Dear Eva,

You are an inspiration to many people and a role model to our generation. Your story touched many people and brought hope back into my life. For the past year and a half my mother has been fighting a severe battle against inflammatory cancer of the breast and liver. ... My mother has undergone surgery, radiation, and she just finished her second session of months of chemotherapy. The doctors informed my family that there is not a lot they can do for her; they can only buy time. In the beginning I possessed an overwhelming hope and I thought that no one could knock it down. I was wrong. I would like to believe what I once did, but I reach into my heart to find it empty. I am tired of living with this burden ... I am tired of fighting this battle. ...When you stood in front of that room and told me your story you inspired me. You gave me hope; you are my hope. My eyes welled up with tears when I realized that God had finally delivered the angel I've been praying for so long. You touched my heart and made me realize that I need faith to survive. Without faith you have nothing. For all the experiences you have been through you possess no hate, only love. You have such a warm heart and a loving soul. ...You gave me the greatest gift of all, the gift of hope ... When my spirits are low and the light starts to fade I'll remember you and your heart of courage. It will be that courage that helps me to move on.

Colleen Crawford (Eastview Secondary School, Barrie)   June 2000

How to Deal with Tragedy

The presentation made by Eva Olsson was very difficult for me to listen to. War is a terrible thing that kills and ruins both during it and long after it's over. It can also create strong and wonderful people like Eva. My grandfather unfortunately did not have that strength.

Mrs. Olsson would have been only five years older than my grandpa was when World War II began. As she was being shipped away on a crowded train where she would lose everything except her sister, my grandpa was being shipped off to boot camp to become part of Hitler Youth.

The terrors each experienced as they were separated from their families, and forced to see and hear things that they could not have even imagined would change each of them forever. Eva experienced terrors of racism; she was a victim of it; my grandfather was brainwashed to be racist — to treat others with little respect, to kill. He learned to hate. He not only was made to brutalize others, but also saw his own family hurt and abused. Eva, although a victim of this racism, did not learn to hate. She lost her family and much of her life to the actions of hateful people; from those actions she learned to love, to never give up hope in mankind.

Mrs. Olsson was able to harness the negative and terrifying experiences and use them to teach others of the dangers of racism. She took something evil and horrible and created a beautiful opportunity to touch the lives of young and old in a positive and helpful way. My grandfather took his hate and negative experiences and allowed them to rule his life. Although he was a successful businessman and a hard-working man, he became an alcoholic. He was violent towards himself and his family; eventually his hate and alcoholism caused him to commit suicide in 1989.

All of us suffer through tragedy; most of us cannot even imagine the horrors suffered by those involved in World War II and the Holocaust. From these two lives we can see the difference in how we deal with our tragic experiences. We can allow them to take us over and fill us with hate, eventually killing us and hurting those around us. Or we can take control of our own lives and make a decision to use our experiences to change the world and make it a better place. I chose the latter. What will you do?

Heidi Rayner (Bracebridge & Muskoka Lakes SS)   February 27, 2000

One and a half million children were annihilated by the Nazis, poisoned in the gas chambers, starved in the concentration camps, or burned alive in the fire pits. Among them were my five little nieces, the most tragic event of my life. Today I am very grateful to have three beautiful grandchildren living next door to me, for they help me find balance in my life.

On March 1, 1995, I was sitting in the family room, with the flames in the woodburning stove making beautiful pictures on the wall. I was watching a video about Winston Churchill that brought back a lot of memories of the concentration camps. My son Jan and two of my grandchildren came in to pick up some bread I'd made, and eleven-year old Brenna was very excited. She had a silver medal on a yellow ribbon around her neck that she had won at a basketball tournament in Muskoka. After they left, I sat thinking about the present and the past, and how blessed I was to have such a lovely family.

My grandchildren call me Bubba. They adore me and it is comforting to have them living right beside me. I am haunted by the memory of my Mama being taken to the gas chamber at Auschwitz holding onto her three little grandchildren. Every time I see my little grandchildren, I count my blessings. My experiences in Auschwitz and Bergen-Belsen make me appreciate many things I might otherwise have taken for granted.

1.

EARLY CHILDHOOD

I was born Ester Malek, in Szatmar into a High Orthodox Hasidic family. When Mama was born in Szatmar it was part of Hungary but after World War I Szatmar became part of Romania. So when I was born Szatmar was part of Romania. I feel my spirit is Romanian — rugged, down-to-earth — and my intellect is Hungarian — attracted to music, art, and philosophy. Either way, I used to call myself Hungarian and speak Hungarian. My father, Haim Ytzhog, was a Hasidic scholar who wrote many religious books, and spent his days studying and teaching at a yeshiva, a Jewish school. My mother, Leah, was a homemaker. There were six children in our family: Sarah, (the eldest), Martin, Regina, me, Lazar, and Fradel (the youngest). My mother said that I was the best baby of all the family. Her feelings probably changed as I grew older.

When my youngest sister, Fradel, was born, I was only 32 months old, but I went to the hospital with my father to see the baby lying in the crib beside my mother's bed. The hospital had a long marble stairway, and I jumped up and down the steps. Fradel had a little head with lots of black hair. Mama wasn't well after this birth, and three months later she had to return to the hospital for surgery. I can still see her sitting on her bed buckling up her high shoes, wearing a beautiful brown coat with a yellow lining. I stood against the bedroom door trying to prevent her from leaving.

Mama told us how disappointed my father was when the doctor told him she was not to have any more children after Fradel was born. Coming out of the doctor's office, my father looked as if somebody had slapped him in the face. They already had six children, but my father wanted as many as possible. His mother had worried because Mama had not had a child in the first two years of their marriage. My grandmother died before her six grandchildren were born.

After Mama had gone to the hospital we sat on the kitchen floor with our backs against the open door and our neighbor, Mrs. Jonas, fed us poppy seed noodles. When I was nine Mrs. Jonas was in the hospital and I went to visit her on my own. I stood by her bedside looking at her arms, which were covered with large brown spots that she had scratched until they bled. I visited her three times, then I was told by her family not to go again, as she had passed away. I wonder now why a nine-year-old felt the need to visit this woman on her deathbed. Was it because she had fed us as small children when our mother was ill?

My Grandfather Jankev (my father's father), whom I loved dearly, lived in the city of Sziget in Romania, in an area formerly known as Northern Transylvania. He sent us a maid to take care of us while my mother was sick, a peasant girl from the Romanian hills. Her clothing, with its layers and layers of skirts, embroidered blouses and lace vest fascinated me. I found out later that she was dismissed because she stole my mother's engagement ring. My grandfather wanted to send another girl but my mother didn't want one, as she felt Sarah was old enough to help out more. We all had to do our share, and I was the "little red hen," the "gofer" as they say now, always running errands, always eager to help. Nothing was too much for me.

Grandfather Jankev made his living sewing the leather tops of custom-made shoes. His family also worked a small farm for their own use. His first wife died at a young age, when my father was about twenty-two. Jankev eventually remarried, to a widow who had a son and daughter about my father's age.

I always loved my grandfather. He was the opposite of my father — generous, caring, lovable and wise. I realize now how important it is for children to have a good male influence around them. My grandfather filled this role for me and my memories of him are all positive. It was a joy to have him visit because he'd play old Yiddish melodies on his violin. He also brought us goodies: lots of walnuts, hazelnuts, and a huge honey cake my step-grandmother would make, as well as a big chunk of homemade butter.

He did not follow the High Orthodox Hasidic way of life that my father practiced. He was very quiet, a pleasant, jolly man always playing around with the kids.

I didn't know my grandfather on my mother's side, not even his name. He owned an egg-grading and export business. My mother told me that he was around 40 when he died in 1905. After he died my Uncle Joseph, my mother's older brother, took over the business. My uncle's business was in a stone building in the market area where the peasants used to bring their eggs to be graded. He would candle them and pack them in crates filled with straw to be exported. My uncle would give us the cracked eggs, which was a big help because sometimes we didn't have money to buy eggs. A lot of eggs were used during the eight-day Passover celebration, added to potatoes to make latkes and other potato casseroles that were eaten as a substitute for bread. I got many bloody knuckles from grating potatoes for latkes. However, eating them made it all worthwhile.

When I was a child I was sent alone to get the cracked eggs. I was really frightened of going inside my uncle's building because it was so dark. I was afraid of the dark; Mama used to warn us not to go out in the dark because the Tartars would steal us away from her. We also bought live poultry at the market and then took it to a kosher slaughterhouse where a qualified person cut the bird's throat and drained the blood. We plucked the bird and burned the last feathers off its skin before we went home.

I enjoyed going to the open market because there were lots of things to see there — people, poultry, fruit and vegetables, flowers, dry goods and even wood for the stove. One day when I was about ten, two or three of us were watching a trapeze artist on a high wire in the market square. As we stood there hypnotized I turned around and saw my father. He had been out looking for us because it was wrong to be out Friday after sundown. We did not get spanked until Saturday night or Sunday morning. Even today I do not understand why a child should have to wait 24 to 48 hours in fear of a future spanking. I think this was sadistic and I cannot see any positive side to it. My father felt that his action was justified because we were late for supper. The fact that we had never seen a trapeze act before and had lost track of time was no excuse. I was never even given a chance to explain.

Once when my father was travelling out of town to different Jewish communities and synagogues promoting his books my mother decided to send me to my Grandfather Jankev's for a little holiday. I was about eleven and a half, and had never been to my grandfather's home, so I eagerly packed my suitcase for the six-hour train trip to Sziget, where my grandparents would pick me up at the station. It was a chance for me to visit my grandfather, my step-grandmother and my father's stepsister, Ester, without the company of any other siblings. However, my father came home before Mama was expecting him and said I could not go. I was so upset I cried all night.

We didn't have a telephone, so we couldn't let my grandparents know I wasn't coming. They waited at the train station for a long time and later they got a letter from my father telling them I wasn't going to go there for that summer holiday. He told them that he was worried that I might fall into the fast moving river near my grandfather's house. I didn't have very good feelings towards my father after that. As it turned out this would have been my only chance to see where my grandparents lived. I never saw Grandfather Jankev again after I turned 18, because his city was emptied of all Jews within 24 hours in the spring of 1944. At that time he would have been around 70 years old. He and his wife were taken to the gas chambers in Auschwitz. I don't know what happened to his stepson and stepdaughter.

Jankev's stepdaughter, Ester, used to visit us from time to time and I remember how beautiful she was. I looked up to her because she did things that were not allowed in our household, like powdering her face. She looked like a Mediterranean Madonna, very tall with outstanding facial features and beautiful clothes. She had a dress made of burgundy lace lined with a hot pink lamé. Lamé was used a lot in Europe at that time, and it had the shiny, slippery feeling of satin. This dress had long tulip-shaped sleeves and I could look right up her arm and see the lining. It was absolutely gorgeous. In 1968, in Canada, I sewed myself an ankle-length dress of burgundy lace, lined it with hot pink satin, and sewed a beautiful belt with a bow and a long sash in the back. I still have that dress today, nicely wrapped up in the closet. I don't know why, but I can not part with it and I look at it from time to time. Perhaps I keep it because I admired Ester so much.

Ester had an older brother who was a very successful businessman and came to visit us only once. My stepuncle looked like a male model who had just stepped out of a men's magazine. Our home only had two rooms so he did not stay overnight in our house. He went to a lavish hotel uptown in the square where the movie house was, but he came during the day to visit and had dinner with us. He wore a beautiful grey suit and a hat to match. My father, his stepbrother, never wore a suit, only an ugly, black robe.

My father only occasionally kept in touch with his stepsister or his stepbrother, because they were ultra-modern and he feared they would have a negative influence on his children. I cannot understand how these children were brought up so modern, so liberal; I would never have known they were Jewish people.

I remember Mama's mother, a very tiny person, short and chubby, who died when she was 76. She lived not too far away from us and I went to visit her when I was about six or seven. She was standing by the stove wearing a wig made out of silk threads. My mother also had a silk wig but wore it only on special occasions.

When I was seven years old I enjoyed going to weddings very much. I had a lot of cousins on my

mother's side of the family, so there were many
weddings, with delicious food and lots of relatives.
Everyone seemed to be happy at the time, but I learned
later that some of them were very unhappy. I enjoyed
my older cousins' visits to our home because they
were allowed to do things that we could not do, like
putting powder on their faces and wearing sheer grey
silk stockings. I found this very confusing. My
Grandfather Jankev was Orthodox and his second
wife was modern, but her children were even more
liberal than their mother was. My mother's older
brother Wolfe was a Hasidic rabbi and his wife was
Orthodox, yet their children were allowed to go to
grade school and had more freedom in their wardrobe
than we did. It was okay for them to show their legs
through their silk stockings and powder their faces.
When I tried to build a friendship with Sarah Ester,
one of my cousins who had quite modern ideas, my
mother discouraged the friendship even though Sarah
Ester was her older brother's daughter. At that time I
was in my midteens and completely confused by the
different religious attitudes within one family. To this
day I do not understand why my parents needed to
carry their beliefs to such extremes.

My mother had four sisters — Fanny, Sarah,
Rosa and Margaret — and four brothers — Yussel,
Ythok, Wolfe, and Jankev. I always looked forward
to visits by my Aunt Margaret, my mother's youngest
sister. One time she brought her two daughters, Ester
and Yentla. Aunt Margaret bought me my first earrings
when I was two months old, and I had them until the

Germans arrived. My Aunt Rosa, Mama's second youngest sister, had no children and loved to be around her older sister's children. She used to tell us jokes. I treasure these memories, but for a while they were overshadowed by my anger at my father's denial and suppression of my needs and ambitions.

My parents' first "apartment," where I was born, was really no more than a winterized shed, with one room, one door and one window. When I was about ten years old I went back there and I could not believe that two adults and four children had lived in it. I asked myself many times why my father had not allowed my mother to continue her dressmaking trade while he spent his time at the synagogue. When Mama's father died she was 11 years old and her brothers bought her a sewing machine. She started sewing beautiful gowns for other women and built this up into a dressmaking business with 11 young women assisting her. My father did not allow her to continue with her profession after their marriage. Was it better for us to live in poverty, with Mama at home and pregnant, than to have her be the breadwinner? I don't know how many years passed before my father earned a living from teaching. When I remember six of us living in one room and later eight of us living in two rooms I understand why a sense of space is so important to me now.

About six years later we moved into two large rooms in an old house, with five of us sleeping in one room and Fradel sleeping with Mama in my parents' bedroom, which had two beds. When we had the maid, she slept on a straw mattress on the floor of our room. As my brothers got older it was more difficult to share one bedroom, as there was no privacy. My parents' room served as their bedroom, as well as being the living room and dining room. The cooking, baking, laundry and sewing were done in our room. When visitors came we had to give up our bed and sleep on the floor. Sometimes visitors stayed as long as four weeks. There was no indoor plumbing, just one outdoor privy for 19 people. Water had to be brought in from the pump and when the pump was dry we had to go two blocks to the square to get water. In those days, I guess, that wasn't so unusual.

The two-room apartment had a lovely porch that faced our garden. My brothers dug the flowerbeds and my sisters and I shaped them and planted pansies, petunias, snapdragons, carnations, aster and geraniums. The porch gave us a little more breathing room, some extra space where we children could play, rain or shine, in the summer. I used to stand on the porch beside my mother, watching as she sewed beautiful tablecloths. It was very delicate work, known as Madeira or eyelets. She cut out the different-shaped holes with tiny scissors. She made a tablecloth for each of the children, large enough to cover a table set for twelve. My mother showed us many other beautiful needlework items she had made for our trousseaux and tucked away in the linen wardrobe.

In the wintertime she saved all the duck and

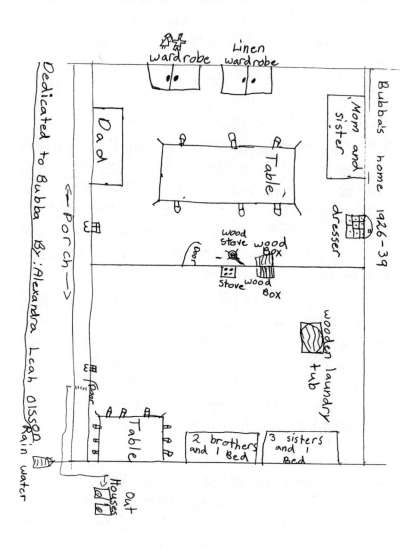

geese feathers that the family and neighbours gathered and separated the down from the rest of the feather. This down was used to make pillows and comforters for our trousseaux as well. Mama showed us a big roll of tea towels, as yet uncut, that my father's mother had woven to be divided later for us children. Unfortunately, none of us ever got to use these beautiful items.

She also showed us her wedding gown, which she had sewn herself. When I asked her why it was pale blue, not white, she said that World War I had not yet ended and she didn't want to be married in a white dress. Perhaps the blue dress was her way of grieving for those killed in the war. The war ended a few months after she married.

My father must have fallen head over heels in love with my mother and accepted her religious way of living. My mother used to tell us kids how much more religious our father became after their marriage. My father was not raised in a Hasidic environment, so it was all right for him to fall in love. My parents appeared to be well matched in spite of being an arranged marriage.

When I was eight years old I had dark, curly hair, dark brown eyes, a slim build, and I was full of energy, eager to help, with an inquisitive mind. Our two-room apartment was in a house that had been converted into four apartments around a courtyard. The Jonas family and the Hermans and another old lady, whom we called Aunt Rosa, along with her daughter and son-in-law, occupied the rest of the complex. None of them were High Orthodox Hasidic Jews. The Jonases gave me goodies for running errands. When I was eleven years old their daughter Fage taught me how to cut and shape my nails. I had never seen a manicure before.

Only a door separated us from the Jonas family's home, and my father put a wardrobe that was nine feet high and six feet wide against the door. Our clothes were stored in there, but my Uncle Joseph often used it to hide from his wife, who was verbally abusive to him and their family. I can still hear her voice as she ran about looking for Joseph, shouting all the time. Their marriage was not a love match like the rest of Mama's family. It had been an arranged marriage and many of these marriages were most unhappy.

2.

HOME LIFE

Once every year a man in a uniform came to the door to ask if there were any school-aged children in the home. Our mother told us to hide in the wardrobe before she opened the door. I can still hear my mother saying, "No, there are no school-aged children here." Following their Hasidic beliefs, my parents did not send their children to public schools. The boys attended *hider* (a Jewish school) only. The tutors who schooled Hasidic girls had a very limited amount of schooling themselves. We learned all about the very limited Hasidic world but were denied contact with others and knowledge of the world outside. We were taught from childhood that females existed for bearing babies and doing household chores. We were first tutored in Yiddish from age six to age nine or ten. We spoke only Yiddish in our home, as speaking Hungarian was considered goyish (gentile). Outside the home we had a choice of speaking either Hungarian or Romanian, and I chose to speak Hungarian, never Romanian. Although we were taught that our "tongues would be cut out" if we lied, we saw our parents lie when it suited their fundamentalist beliefs.

When I was around ten years of age I was sent to summer school where I was taught some Hungarian and more Yiddish. The school was a large converted home that had been donated by the Jewish community for the purpose of teaching underprivileged children in the summer. At this beautiful summer school I felt deprived and cheated because I wanted a full public education, not a narrow, self-interested and restricted education. I became resentful to the point that I was not interested in learning what they were teaching. The more summer school I attended, the more I resented my parent's way of living and their beliefs. On the positive side, I enjoyed the outdoor gym activities. After gym class we would go inside and get hot milk and sour dough rye bread, which I liked very much (and still do). Then we had some lessons, followed by lunchtime at which we were given soup — either bean, goulash, or potato — and bread. After lunch we went outside for recess and played in the big orchard that was part of the property. We used to stuff ourselves with all kinds of fruit.

Near the orchard was a military hospital that treated World War I shell-shocked veterans. There were bars on the windows to prevent people from getting out. I remember one man sitting on the windowsill holding his knees to his chest and just staring in front of him. The children said this was a hospital for *bolond ember,* crazy people. Today it would be called a mental institution. Seeing this building and its occupants every day was sometimes frightening.

My mother's oldest sister Fanny used to travel long distances from market to market to sell her dry goods, while the men prayed all day in the synagogue. She rented a horse and an open wagon and travelled day or night, regardless of the weather, to get to the next market. My sister Sarah and I went with my aunt on one of her trips. We were hoping to sell textile remnants, but it was so bitterly cold and wet that the market was empty and we sold nothing that day. We left in the afternoon and travelled home, where we told our mother what this journey was like. We told her that we would never again make that trip. Until then my mother had no idea how hard her sister was working to provide a living for her family of eight children. My aunt never complained; she was too busy.

My Aunt Fanny and her husband were well-to-do compared to us and when they visited us during Hanukkah my uncle would give the children *gelt* (money) to buy candy. Once when we were visiting them for a celebration in honour of her son's upcoming wedding, a funny incident happened. As the guests arrived, Fanny decided to heat up another room by lighting the stove there. Lighting fires is forbidden for Jews on the Sabbath, so a gentile lady was called to do this. This lady saw that there was already scrap paper in the stove, so she lit the fire. Suddenly my cousin shouted, "The gelt!" Apparently my aunt hid her money, thousands of bills (*pengo*), wrapped up in old newspapers, in the pot-bellied stove. Since Orthodox Jews are forbidden to touch money on the Sabbath, the only person who could rescue the money was the lady who lit the fire, and she was able to rescue some of it. The room was full of smoke so we kids ran out and played in the yard.

Uncle Wolfe , my mother's brother, visited us from time to time. He called me *Cigainer* (Gypsy), and gave me pennies, which I used to buy a slice of Dobos Tarta, my favourite cake at the bakery. It is a yellow eight-layer cake, cocoa-covered, with butter filling and carmelized butterscotch icing. I would make sure it was gone before I got home. I never stayed around to see if he gave pennies to my brothers or sisters. Perhaps he favoured my Gypsy appearance and gave the pennies to me first.

Aunt Rosa, a modern Jewish woman, bought me a white chrysanthemum for my tenth birthday. My mother wondered why she would do that, as Hasidic people don't celebrate birthdays. I was very surprised but pleased to receive a gift on my birthday, and chrysanthemums are still my favorite flowers.

I know some of Mama's family fought in the war but I don't know how many. Many Jews fought in the First World War, some with the Allies and some with the Germans. Those who fought with the Germans in World War I thought they would be protected in World War II, but Hitler had different ideas. My Uncle Joseph still carried a bullet from World War I in his arm when he was taken to the gas chamber in Auschwitz.

3.

ADOLESCENCE AND REBELLION

I was 14 when we rented a bungalow a block away from our two-room apartment. This place had been owned by Mr. Lefcovich, an elderly gentleman who used to sit outside in the summer watching us go to the square to get water. Soon after, my parents sent me to stay overnight with an old lady we called Záli Néni, who lived a block away. They told me she was very sick, but actually she was dying. I guess they didn't want to tell me the truth because I was so young. It is a Jewish belief that a person should not die alone, so I slept there every night for a week and in the morning an older woman arrived to stay with her during the day. However, I was a sheltered 14-year-old, and the sounds of her dying are still with me today. One morning the older woman left a few minutes after she had arrived, and I didn't know why. An hour later she returned with ten men, a *minion,* required by Jewish rites to say the prayers for the dead. Then I knew Záli had died during the night.

What was my parents' motive in sending me

rather than my older sister Sarah to be with a dying woman? Were my parents unaware of the fear and pain I would feel? Did they think I was the strongest of my siblings? If so, why did they not reinforce this rather than trying to make me docile? Perhaps I was the natural choice because I was the "little red hen" who could be counted on to get things done. This incident had a profound effect on me and I still have a hard time dealing with it, even after all the atrocities that I have witnessed and endured since then.

As I entered my teens my father was very concerned about me. I had my own ideas as to how far one should take religion and I feel my parents went overboard. Hasidic females had to wear long, thick black stockings, and dresses with long sleeves and high necks. They couldn't look out the window because a boy might see them. Their marriages were arranged through a matchmaker, and they met the boy for the first time when their parents met his. They got to see him for a half an hour and that marriage was expected to last for the rest of their lives. I still feel it's like throwing a piece of meat to the wolves, because there is no love.

In spite of all this, I had respect for my parents while I was still living under their roof. A turning point in my life came when I was sixteen because I had to choose between following my parents' wishes and developing my own identity. I chose not to have confrontations with them because I respected their right to have their beliefs and I realized they were not going to bend. They chose the way they wanted to live, perhaps because that's what they were taught and they didn't know how to be any more liberal. They forbade me to go across the street to our neighbour's, who had a radio and read movie magazines. These neighbours were liberal and my parents did not want me to get any modern ideas or read literature that would not agree with their conservative views. Being a teenager, I found it easy to figure out ways around this. When they sent me to do errands, I would go four blocks around the back way to end up in my neighbour's backyard, or go up to the square and stare at the movie house displays with the pictures of the stars. It was all very exciting. It didn't take my father long to figure out why it took me so long to go anywhere, and they kept a very close watch on me. However, I had to do what I had to do. I suppose, having such strong convictions, they also had to do what they had to do. Because of my need to get out, I never said no when my father or my older sister Regina asked me to run an errand. Since we had no telephone or car, we had to do our errands on foot. Regina never hesitated to say no when she didn't want to go. I, on the other hand, would always agree to go.

One of my chores was to take the dough to the bakery twice a week. The baker's wife, Mrs. Wiess, was no stranger to us, as her mother and my mother grew up in the same courtyard. One day when I returned from the baker my mother asked me why the Wiess family liked me better than my sister Regina, why they thought of me as an "unpolished diamond."

Since I was fifteen at the time, how could I answer that question? I knew I was more open, friendly and helpful. I wondered if the Weiss family could see something in me that my parents' religious beliefs prevented them from seeing. My parents could not understand how Ester could be liked more than her older sister, how she could be an unpolished diamond when she caused them so much trouble.

I realized even at that young age that it was to my advantage to go on errands because that gave me a chance to mix with other people and hear what was going on outside the Hasidic environment. I wanted more exposure to the outside world and I was very happy to go there. There was a lovely park uptown with beautiful things to see: an opera house, and a theatre showcasing movies and movie stars. Beside the theatre was a large hotel, inside which were large black leather chairs, elegant table settings, and chandeliers. In the back of the hotel was a refreshment booth where I would buy lemon sherbet. One afternoon my curiosity got the better of me and I went into the opera house, through a door left open while the cleaners were working. The beautiful red velvet drapes and upholstered chairs amazed me. Even the balcony was red and gold.

Eventually my curiosity got me into trouble. One Sunday afternoon my cousins Rachael and Ester and I decided to go and watch the children's puppet show, "Saint Mikulas," which took place behind the hotel. When my father found out where I had been I was severely disciplined. I found out later that neither of my cousins was spanked.

My brother Lazar was one and a half years younger than I was and we both felt that our parents took their religious beliefs too far. However, we never talked about any of this in front of our parents. When he walked on the street he used to tuck his side curls under his hat. I saw him do this myself, but my father never saw it. He was about 16 years old at the time, tall, handsome, and well built, with blonde hair and blue eyes. Lazar had been seeing a girl in our neighbourhood for about three years without my parents' knowledge. One time he took my new cardigan and gave it to her as a present. He was very much in love with her and he knew I would not complain or tell my parents. He became the other black sheep in the family because he had to sneak around to see his girl friend.

Evening prayers at the synagogue were important to my father, and Lazar usually went with him. One day my father asked Lazar which synagogue he had been at the night before. Lazar said that he had gone to a different synagogue. My father did a little detective work and checked each synagogue in the area to see if anyone had seen my brother. I realized that Lazar had gone to the movies with his girlfriend, not to evening prayers. Father confronted my brother, demanding to know where he had been. Lazar insisted that he had gone to prayers. Father punished Lazar very severely, hitting him many times. I can still hear Lazar saying, "My God, why am I being punished?" Finally my brother banged his fist on the table and said, "The more you hit me, the more determined I am to go to the movies." Maybe that's the difference between a boy and a girl: He really stood up to my father, whereas I would have said nothing. I don't know whose reaction to my father was the right one, my brother's or mine.

However, when I was about 16 years old I did confront my father for the first time. He arrived home at noon from the synagogue and was telling my mother a tragic story about a Jewish family whose daughter and her gentile boyfriend were found shot dead in a cornfield. My father was very upset by this tragic event. I felt he should not be discussing this incident in front of the children and I confronted him, saying, "It's not up to us to talk about other people's problems." He was shocked into silence at my remarks. But what angered me most was that two young people were dead because they loved each other and their parents' religious beliefs got in the way. The girl's parents would not accept the gentile boyfriend, so the couple saw suicide as their only option. My father must have sensed that my attitude was maturing in a different direction than he would have liked. He became more suspicious of my different beliefs about freedom and privacy, and my growing independence. Some days I used to walk around in a daze wondering what it would be like living in another environment. I was very unhappy in my surroundings because I had great difficulty accepting my parents' narrow attitude. As I became older my need to have the freedom to choose became stronger and stronger and caused my father more stress.

I believed then, and I still believe 53 years later, that if my father had been able to communicate differently with Lazar and me, my views of him and his religion might be different today. He could have encouraged Lazar to go to early prayer and go to the movie afterward, but my father wasn't capable of that. If Lazar had been allowed some freedom he would not have gone behind my father's back.

Once when Grandfather Jankev came to visit, I was so excited I ran to Lazar's school to tell him. His rabbi spanked him because he wanted to leave. He ran out anyway and was spanked again when he got home. I felt guilty for the punishment he had received and was very careful from then on not to cause him more pain.

I compare this situation to the shaping of a tree. As the branches grow in different directions they should be supported and not forced back toward the trunk. Each branch must be supported with care; otherwise it may break off from the main trunk. My parents were not supportive of Lazar or me.

In 1942 my brother-in-law needed a piece of paper to prove that his grandfather had paid taxes, so I was sent on a seven-hour train trip to Debrecen at the age of 17. This was only my second trip out of town. I was to stay with an Orthodox Jewish family who owned a delicatessen and provided my meals. The first evening I was there I went out, and the feeling of freedom, of being on my own, was overwhelming. I looked for a bus and asked the driver where there was a movie theatre. He told me to go to the end of the line to the Opera House. I don't remember the name of the movie but I do remember the story. I especially remember the love scene in the swimming pool by the garden. Being so young and naive I had never been in this situation myself, but it was thrilling to watch. I went straight back to my room afterwards, fantasizing and thinking about all the beautiful love scenes. This experience at the theatre hit me like a lightning bolt, and stimulated emotions and physical sensations that were all new to me. I wished I had someone to hug and kiss and make love to me that way. Although I asked myself why I had these feelings and wondered if they were normal, I knew then that I liked these feelings very much. Why wasn't I told that girls can have such feelings and taught how to deal with them? These feelings did not last, but the memory of them did. Of course I could not share this experience with my mother or my sisters. The environment I grew up in suppressed all sexual feelings. We were never exposed to romantic love because Hasidic marriages are arranged without love entering the picture. Perhaps love comes later for them, I don't know.

It was probably fortunate that no male companion was involved in my movie experience because I would have been completely vulnerable to his advances. It is said that ignorance is bliss but in this instance my ignorance could have caused a disaster: pregnancy and being denounced by my family.

The next morning, after I picked up my brother-in-law's papers at the Registry Office, I took the train home. My father called me outside and confronted me with information about what I had been doing while I was away. He must have gone to the post office, telephoned the people with whom I stayed and had them spy on me. He hit me, slapped me in the face, verbally abused me, and kicked me with his boots. He always wore knee-high leather boots with his black trousers tucked in them. It was very degrading to be beaten in such a way and I felt I was going to collapse. I denied doing any wrong, never admitting to him that I had gone to a movie. The beating went on for about two hours, outside in the yard behind a high fence where we couldn't be seen. I have asked myself many times why he beat me in the yard and not inside the house. Obviously he did not want to discipline me in front of my siblings. I had been spanked many times inside the house, often being hit with his belt while I lay across his lap, but this was a much more vicious beating and it took place outside the house. Could it be that he wanted to maintain a gentle father image with my siblings? Could it be he feared his other children would lose faith in his teachings? It went on until my mother opened the door and said, "Haim Ytzhog, enough. This is enough now."

I lost all respect for my father because of this degrading treatment of me, all done in the name of his religion. I consider it lucky that I don't hate men as a result. I never had a chance to work things out with my father because my family was annihilated in the war. I am not even sure if it would have been possible. He died of starvation in a concentration camp in December 1944. Perhaps I feared my father because of what I saw as his irrational behaviour and discipline. I never loved my father, but I have released him so that his soul may rest in peace. By doing so, I have regained my peace as well.

I was very quiet for weeks after being beaten by my father, crying myself to sleep at night. I avoided any contact, even eye contact, with my father. My parents couldn't reach me, so I was put on the train and sent to my Aunt Sarah's home in Hungary for a few weeks. Sarah's first husband had been killed in World War I and she had later married a man who had five children. Two of my stepcousins met me at the station with open arms and we walked to their home. My aunt was on the porch waiting to greet me. Their home, which they rented from their Hungarian neighbours, was very large and had a clay floor. The neighbours also owned a vineyard some distance outside the village and a couple of weeks after my arrival they asked Aunt Sarah if I could walk with them to the vineyard. My Aunt Sarah showed more faith and trust in me than my parents had ever done, and I made that trip many times.

During one of those visits to the vineyard it rained heavily as I walked home. My curly hair hung to my shoulders as I walked barefoot back to the house. It was a very hot day, so I was only wearing a very thin navy blue crimpoline dress covered with flowers, which my mother had made. Every curve of my body showed through the wet dress, making me very aware of my physical attributes, which I had never acknowledged at home. The landlord's son had arrived home from university, where he was studying to be a gynecologist, and he saw me arrive home soaking wet.

When I went outside after dinner he called me over to his porch. We sat on the edge of the porch talking until midnight. Sitting and having a conversation with someone of the opposite sex was a whole new experience for me. He described the lifestyle he enjoyed on the university campus in Debrecen. I listened with amazement and envy as he told me about his friends and the courses he was taking to get his degree in medicine. He also shared with me the differences between living in a big city and the small village where he grew up. He told me he enjoyed working in their vineyard and orchard.

I was just seventeen and I did not feel comfortable talking to him about my home environment. I didn't want him to know how ashamed I was of not having an education, so I was a very good listener. When I did talk, it was about the fruit in the orchard, the grapes in the vineyard, and the weather. At some point I became aware that I was responding to his unaccustomed closeness. I felt he might have kissed me had my Aunt Sarah not shown up on the porch when she did. This could never have happened at home. In spite of (or because of) my father's strictness I longed for the kind of connection that had happened on that porch.

Lazar wrote me that he had overheard my parents talking about me. Apparently my father was bothered by the fact that I had just accepted his punishment and not talked back to him.

About a week after I arrived at my Aunt Sarah's home, my stepcousin Yidu sneaked away from the Hungarian Army barracks for the weekend. When we met there was an instant mutual attraction. Much to my surprise Yidu was seated next to me at the table for Friday night dinner. At our home the males sat on one side and the females sat on the other, never together. Even though I was over 17 I had never sat next to a man at the table, not even my father. I felt my leg touch Yidu's leg under the table. I was not startled because of what I had seen in movies. In fact I welcomed the ecstasy of contact. When he moved even closer I responded because I shared his feelings. After we left the dinner table Yidu and I talked for quite some time on the porch. He told me about the army and I spoke to him of my home life and how different it was from his. At dinner on Saturday we sat very close to each other once again. He had to leave in the morning and sneak back into the barracks. He asked permission to write to me and I gave him the address of my neighbour across the street from my home.

I left for home about two weeks after Yidu had returned to the barracks. At home, I didn't speak to my father for the longest time. I spoke to my mother and the rest of the family (except for Lazar) only when I was spoken to. Shortly after I arrived home I received a short letter from Yidu describing how he had sneaked over the fence back into camp and promising to write to me again soon. The second letter was more personal and intimate, describing his feelings for me. He knew that his army unit would be sent as slave labor to the front in the Ukraine, but wasn't sure when it would happen. In other letters he spoke of his wish for us to get together after the fighting. Sadly, I had to tear each letter to pieces because I could not let my family know about them. I wonder what punishment I would have received from my father had he known about our secret commitment.

Later, when Mama and I were talking about marriage, I told her that Yidu was the man I wanted to marry. She agreed that her sister had fine stepchildren, but her main concern was what my children would wear if their father didn't wear the Hasidic habit — the streimel (a fur hat) and a long black caftan (a robe) — on the Sabbath and holidays. My happiness didn't matter as much to her as what other Hasidic Jews would think.

I received two or three more letters from Yidu over the next few months. In the fall of 1942 he was moved to Kiev and the letters stopped. Later we heard the Germans had destroyed Kiev. There were no more letters.

4.

MAMA

In spite of our different views of how much religion should control our lives, I always felt close to Mama. I know she suffered a lot of pain with headaches and high blood pressure caused by major surgery she had after Fradel was born. Even as a young child I seemed to have a natural empathy for pain and suffering. Perhaps that is why I felt so close to my mother. She used to get up very early in the morning to start her sewing, and I would stand opposite her and work the pedal of the old Singer sewing machine.

Monday and Friday mornings she would get up and make the dough for bread, which was a staple in our diet. Boiled potatoes were grated into the rye flour in a long wooden container, and yeast, salt and water were added. When I heard Mama in the kitchen, I would get up and help her knead the dough. I remember her telling me many times to keep kneading until my hands were clean. We would let the dough rise until it doubled in size, then shape it in two-foot long or one-and-a-half-foot round loaves and take them to the bakery to be baked. Two hours later Regina and I would return to the baker's to pick up the bread.

On Friday we baked challah, a braided egg loaf. I loved to braid the challah and had learned to do this when I was eight or ten. I used to braid six miniature challahs, one for each child. We also made sweet breads, cinnamon rolls, and walnut crescents for the Sabbath. Friday was always a very busy day, as it took practically all day to prepare the food for the Sabbath. We cooked a fish dish entree, chicken soup, and hot desserts, either rice with prunes or stewed carrots. Sometimes we would have honey cake. All this preparation was a lot of work but the results were so good to eat.

The casseroles, including the big pot of chicken soup, had to be kept hot for the evening meal. Because no fires could be lit on Friday after sundown, the only way to do this was to place the dishes between big pillows on the bed (to keep them from tipping) and then cover them with the down comforter. They would stay hot until my father and two brothers came home from the synagogue. In mid-afternoon we had to prepare the Sabbath lunch and take it to the baker's to be cooked. This lunch was usually cholent, a well-known Jewish dish that is a complete meal in a pot. The ingredients include brown beans, potatoes, onions, seasoning and a piece of meat, including the bone. Sometimes a large dumpling covers the bottom of the pot. Mama would usually make a larger dumpling in a separate pot because there would often be ten of us to feed if my father brought students home for lunch.

When this was all prepared we put it in a metal box that had been custom-made to hold two large pots. In the late afternoon we would carry it to the baker who placed it in the oven with many other families' cholent. It would cook slowly overnight and we would pick it up the next day after the baker returned from the synagogue. His oven was coal-fired and would not need to be lit on the Sabbath. Challah was baked from early morning till mid-afternoon on Friday before the oven was filled with cholent.

We also carried a pail of coals home from the baker on Mondays, swinging the pail so the coals would stay hot. We used the coals in the iron to press many white shirts and linens. I hated ironing and starching all those white shirts.

During the hot summer, we would eat Sabbath Day chicken. On Fridays Mama would cook chicken paprikash or fried young chicken that was eaten with a fruit compote and challah. Since we had no refrigeration we lowered the perishable food into the well to keep it cool until it was served. Chicken was the most popular meat because chickens could be raised on a small plot of land, unlike beef.

My mother taught me a lot of things, some positive and some negative. She taught me how to be resourceful, how to be a good homemaker, how to cook and bake. I saw how caring she was, especially when she made pretty dresses for us. She was a very devoted person. The one negative trait that stands out in my mind was her inability or

unwillingness to discipline us when she felt we needed
it. If my father were out of town for four or five
weeks we would have to wait for his return to be
punished. It got to the point that I used to fear my
father's return and view him as a villain. Sometimes I
even wished that he would never come back. I
resented my mother's decision not to deal with me
promptly because it made me feel so negative toward
my father. Her behavior also demonstrated to us that
she was a weaker parent than my father.

I have asked myself many times if my father
really enjoyed punishing Lazar or me when he came
home from a trip or from the synagogue. I never saw
my father lay a hand on or speak a harsh word to
anyone other than the two of us. When the Sabbath
ended, gloom would overcome me as I wondered
what I would be punished for — fixing my hair,
looking out the window, not finishing my prayer book,
sneaking over to my neighbors' home or some trivial
matter that Fradel or one of my other siblings had
reported to our father or mother. My parent's religious
fundamentalism prevented them from seeing that two
of their children needed to live a different way.

During the summer of 1941, when I was 17,
my mother sent me by train to stay with her cousin
for a few weeks on their ten-acre farm. I loved the
farm environment, especially the fresh milk. They
were a modern Jewish family with five children. When
it came time to leave for home I took the afternoon
train. The oldest son, who was married, travelled part
of the way with me. When we left that train we had to

stay overnight before I caught another train in the morning. We shared a large room that had two separate beds. When the room was dark and I was in bed, my cousin lifted my cover and tried to get in bed with me. I pushed him away, saying, "No! Why are you here?" He answered, "Every man needs two wives!" He did leave, but I could not sleep for fear he would come back.

Why was I never made aware that such things could happen? My parents made sure I knew all about their Hasidic beliefs, but taught me nothing about spiritual, moral and sexual values. I was taught that going to the movies was forbidden, but I knew nothing about much more important aspects of life. Yet if something had happened that night and I had become pregnant, they would have cast me out of my family as a disgraced unwed mother.

When young men came from out of town to study with my father at the yeshiva, my father couldn't call home and tell us to set another plate because we had no telephone. He'd just show up at the door and say, 'Leah, put another plate or two on the table." It was never a problem. We just shared what we had. When the young man's parents couldn't afford to pay my father for teaching, they'd send staple goods such as flour, wine, eggs, whatever was available. I remember my father surprised my mother once with an aluminum wash bucket in which we could boil our clothes on the stove. Not everyone on our street had a boiling pot, so it traveled up and down the street to whoever needed it.

5.

SARAH'S WEDDING

When my older sister Sarah was married, 400 invitations were sent out because my father was very well known in the Hasidic community. Sarah was beautiful, with long black hair that was shaved off the morning after the wedding, following Hasidic tradition. Mama's second cousin Zelda came a week before the wedding and did all the baking and cooking. Zelda made her living cooking and baking for wealthy people. On the wedding day Sarah, Mama and father had to fast all day.

In the early afternoon Mama dressed Sarah all in white. Then Sarah sat in a big chair surrounded by beautiful flowers and the female guests stepped up and congratulated her on her upcoming marriage. This went on all afternoon. The groom and the male guests were in a different room. Large trays of honey cake and yellow cake were passed around and there were also small glasses of plum brandy for the adult guests.

My father gave my mother a signal to get Sarah ready. Regina and I removed all the bobby pins from her hair, letting her hair hang loose. We also removed any safety pins that remained in her dress. After that my mother and the groom's mother took Sarah by the arms and led her out under the canopy where the groom and the guests were waiting. She was led seven times around the groom and then stood beside him. My father performed the marriage ceremony as the guests stood with lit candles in their hands.

The reception was held in a large hall behind the synagogue. The groom sat beside Sarah until all the food was eaten, but when the music started to play he left the table and joined the men on the other side of the hall. My father had the first dance with the bride, each of them holding one end of a handkerchief, never making physical contact. The groom danced with Sarah the same way; then he joined the men and the women started to dance.

As in most families, not all siblings got along with each other, for various reasons. We didn't fight, but we were usually working and didn't have time to play together the way other children did. My sister Fradel, the baby of the family, would tell my parents if I did anything unorthodox on the Sabbath, and I would be spanked the next day.

My brother Martin got married through a matchmaker in 1942 and everything seemed okay because we had not been affected by the war yet. A marriage was arranged through a matchmaker in 1943 for my sister Regina, but the situation was different. The German army was getting closer so my parents decided to have a quiet ceremony. All our close relatives were invited but not the people from my father's congregation. The bride and groom did not have an apartment to go to so they had to use my parent's bedroom.

In spite of the war, going on Regina was preoccupied with the purification rituals during the week before the marriage. My mother talked to her secretly about her wedding night duties and about purification. After each menstruation, women had to go to the *mikvah*, a part of the bathhouse, where a female attendant — a *rabbinette* —checked for stains and decided from the cloth whether or not the woman was clean and could continue having sexual relations with her husband.

At breakfast the day after the wedding, I saw Regina pick up the salt and pepper shakers and place them between her and her husband, indicating to him that she was not pure for him after the wedding night because there was a bloodstain on the sheets. Only when I was older did I understand the idea of separate beds. We were never told anything about sexual relationships until the week before the wedding. What gives men the right to impose such laws on their wives? For whose benefit was this law imposed? I cannot see the connection between these rituals and religion. I feel it would be a burden to have to deal with these different rituals.

My parents were worried that I would never get married because I was so thin, so they made me put on two pairs of flannel bloomers and gave me more food to eat, hoping to fatten me up. My father infuriated me by trying to marry me off to a young student from his yeshiva, a young man with pitch-black hair, a beard, side curls, and long, black clothes. This happened while I was still secretly receiving letters from Yidu. I stood up to my father and told him that if he forced me to marry this man, I would leave my husband, come home and cry on my father's head. My Aunt Margaret, my mother's younger sister, was my mentor and encouraged me to stand up to my father on this matter. Her father had died when my mother was only 11, so the brothers took control of the family, especially the five girls. The brothers married my Aunt Margaret off to a man she didn't even like, and she was very often unhappy. She never forgave them for forcing this horrible man on her.

Aunt Margaret helped me to become the person that I am today. She came the week before Regina's wedding to help bake and cook, as we didn't have a caterer. While we were walking up to the square with all the beautiful shops to pick up something we needed for the wedding, she said, "Esther, don't let them do to you what they did to me." It is written in the Torah that a marriage must be a love match. Parents were not allowed to force a loveless marriage to take place, but that's what often happened. However, I got out of it that time.

My sister Sarah was not happy in her arranged marriage. She had three children in four years and complained to our Mama that her husband spent all his time in the synagogue while she baked bread and cakes for the wealthy neighbors. My father gave

Sarah's husband pep talks about helping his wife more often but they had no effect. Sometimes I would help Sarah with the heavier loads.

My parents were devastated when Sarah became very ill in the fall of 1943. The doctors were unable to diagnose her illness, so my father and I took her by ambulance to Budapest, a six-hour drive. My mother stayed at home with Sarah's three children, who were aged one to three, plus her own family. Sarah's husband was in hiding from the army or the Germans and no one knew where he was. My father prayed and paced the floor, offering his own life in exchange for Sarah's. I knew her struggle was over when they called a *minion* to give her last rites. On January 11, 1944, after ten days in the hospital, my oldest sister, Sarah, died of encephalitis, leaving three little girls and no father around to take care of them. My dad sent my mother a telegram, saying that we were coming home and would have to leave my sister in the sanatorium. He could not tell her of Sarah's death. Sarah was buried that same day in Budapest, following Jewish tradition. We cried on the train ride home, wondering how we were going to face her children. When we got home I could see in my mother's face that she knew Sarah had died. My mother cried terribly. We mourned Sarah's death in the traditional Jewish way by sitting on the floor for seven days (*shiva*). We covered the mirrors, dipped hard-boiled eggs in ashes and ate them, and made cuts on our coat lapels.

My mother's younger sister, Rosa, arrived

from Romania to be with her. Rosa had no children of her own and visited us twice a year to be around the children. She was a fun person to be with, always telling us jokes and funny stories about her youth.

Just as things were starting to get better for us, my father gave up teaching and spent all his time working on his books. We even did the bookbinding at home. My mother made glue on the stove out of flour and water. We cut the sheets of paper and put everything in numerical order. Sometimes I went with him to the printing house, where the typesetting fascinated me. We were poor, so we worked very hard to make a little income any way we could, including selling textiles from the house. Lazar had 40 Angora rabbits that he shaved twice a year. Fradel spun the wool and we sold it to a man who manufactured sweaters, scarves and hats. My older brother Martin and I made beautiful Persian rugs at home. A man supplied us with a large frame, wool, and a pattern, and we tied knots on the frame following the pattern. This was my only social contact with Martin, as he was usually at the synagogue praying with my father.

One day in February 1944 I had severe stomach pains and my parents took me to the doctor. He gave us "pills" which I swallowed and which made me even sicker. My parents had never seen suppositories before and didn't know how to administer them. My neighbors across the street saw how sick I was and took me to a second doctor, who realized that my appendix had burst and removed it.

6.

GERMAN OCCUPATION

In the early 1940s my father came home and told us shocking stories that he had heard at the synagogue or read in the Jewish newspapers. A Polish man who had escaped from Poland came to my father's synagogue and told him that when the Germans arrived in Poland in 1939 they went to a Jewish home, took the male head of the household out and made him dig a big grave. He was forced to bury his family of nine alive and pour lye on them. Then they shot him and threw him in the grave. Soldiers who saw pregnant women on the street stabbed them in the stomach with their bayonets.

In 1940 the Germans occupied Romania. In the beginning the Romanian collaborators seized 40,000 homes and property from Jewish families and handed them to non-Jews. The Romanians had started to kill Jews before the SS or the Gestapo arrived. My father was very concerned, as he had relatives in Ploesti, near Bucharest.

My parents tried to shelter us by not telling us everything that was going on, but I kept my ears open and became more frightened as I found out

more. Some Jews began leaving for Israel, but my
father said we couldn't go there because my mother
had high blood pressure and couldn't take the heat.
My mother said she envied my late sister Sarah because she had had a proper burial. It was as if she
knew what lay ahead for the rest of the family. My
sister's little girls were very sad, especially Judy, who
was three at the time. One day she found the belt of
her mother's dress on the floor and she recognized
it. She picked it up and hugged it, saying, "Mama,
Mama's dress."

In late February 1944, we heard at the railway
station that freight trains containing thousands of Jews
were passing through our town. Lazar and I started
going to people's homes late at night and collecting
food. We took the food by horse and buggy to the
station, hoping that the people who owned the hotel
beside the railway station could get the food to the
people on the trains.

One night a woman on one of the freight trains
asked me to take her baby. I took it into the hotel,
gave it a bath, wrapped it in its little blanket and
returned to the train. But the mother denied that I had
taken the baby from her and refused to take it back.
Nobody else wanted to take that child back onto the
train either. They must have known something that
we didn't. Finally I gave it to an older woman on the
train.

My brother and I worked very hard. We didn't
care whether we were tired or not; we were running
on adrenaline. We knew something was very wrong,

and we felt compelled to do something. Although it was unusual for young people to be out all night, my parents said nothing. My father came home from the synagogue one day, pleased that the people from his congregation had heard what his son and daughter were doing and approved. One man told my dad that we should eat *hazer* (pork) to give us extra strength, suggesting that this would be acceptable for such a good reason.

On March 19, 1944 the Germans marched into Hungary and into our hometown. My parents were scared to let us walk on the street because the SS, Hitler's murderers, were everywhere. The Gestapo went into Jewish banks and businesses demanding money, jewelry, and valuable possessions. The Hungarian police collaborated with the Gestapo by identifying Jewish homes. Community leaders were taken as hostages by the Gestapo and threatened with death unless they gave the Germans all they wanted. It was too late to fight back or deny the Gestapo, as that would have resulted in death on the spot.

They created a ghetto, an area of town where all Jews were forced to live, and our house was inside it. We were horrified to realize that we couldn't go any further than two or three streets from home. Jewish people from the villages were forced to move into the ghetto by April 15, 1944. Every Jewish family in the ghetto had to take people in, and we took in a family of five. Added to the eleven people in our family, this meant that sixteen of us were occupying three rooms and a kitchen and sharing one outdoor privy. However, we got along, sleeping on the floor, and sharing our soup and bread. The population of Jews in the ghetto in Szatmar swelled from 13,000 to 24,000 by May 15, 1944. Food was rationed, and because we were locked in the ghetto, with guards everywhere, we could not go out to buy things anymore.

My brother-in-law decided to hide some valuables under the floor. Our house had no basement, so he dug a hole in the yellow clay and put in a lot of things that were important to him, including precious things that his parents had given him. His parents lived in western Hungary and they had already left the country. When my sister Sarah and I had gone to their home in March of 1943, we had brought a lot of things back with us. All these items were hidden along with Sarah's diamond rings and some other jewelry that my mother and sisters had. Naively, they threw some items onto the roof and into the eavestroughs, where the rain could easily wash them out. We thought we would be returning soon.

I cannot describe the fear on my parent's faces. At that time everyone was very afraid. The sixteen of us lived there for four weeks, until the day a man with a drum came, stood in the square, and read from a piece of paper, "You've got two hours to pack your bags with clothing, no food. You're going to a work camp, a brick factory in Germany."

We packed our bags and lined up with our families, five people to a row. Included in our family group were Sarah's three children and my brother

Martin, his wife, and their little baby. My sister Regina had to stay behind in the ghetto hospital because her six-month-old baby girl had the measles. We learned later that the patients from this hospital were evacuated directly to the gas chamber.

We were marched to the train station where my brother Lazar and I had previously tried to help the people on the freight trains. It took us a long time to get to the station because they took us along the backroads rather than through the city. I guess they didn't want the people to see what was going on, but many Hungarians were lined up along the road as we marched the seven kilometers to the train station and the Hungarian police and military both co-operated with the Germans. I couldn't understand why Hungarians were not only allowing the Germans to do this to us but were also assisting them.

I wondered what the SS were going to do with the children. Children were not allowed to cry, and when they did, the SS beat them and their parents. But children cry and sometimes you can't make them stop. I heard of cases where parents suffocated a child when they covered its mouth to stop it from crying. The Germans crammed 80 to 100 people into each boxcar where there was one pail to be used as a toilet and one pail with drinking water. People were crying, but they had to do so quietly because everyone feared the SS. In the shuffle some parents lost their children. Some older people who were sick before getting in the boxcar died from the heat. Children developed dysentery.

My father just prayed and prayed. My mother was sitting in a corner of the boxcar, holding tightly onto Sarah's three children, with Martin's wife and baby and six other family members beside her. My mother was crying and praying. When I asked her why she was crying, she said, "I'm not crying for me. I'm crying for you, for all of my children. I have lived." She was 49 at the time.

We didn't know exactly where we were going; we had just been told that we were going to Germany to work in a factory. When we reached Kassa the SS took over supervision from the Hungarian army. There were no windows in the boxcar, just one tiny square with iron little bars over it, and we would peek out through that and see the SS hanging onto the side of the train. That horrific journey from Kassa to Auschwitz took about four days. There was no fresh air, no room to move. The smell was sickening. Everyone was crying or praying or both. Seeing the sadness on the faces of the older people caused me to be fearful, they seemed to know something. Sometimes I sat and held one of my nieces in my arms. At other times I listened to Mama saying she had thought she would never have to go through another war. She could not understand why the old people, women and children were being shipped to work in Germany. There was very little conversation among the human cargo; they feared what the SS might do if they heard them talking. We slept leaning against each other, exhausted and starved for oxygen. If there is a hell it was in that boxcar.

7.

AUSCHWITZ

We arrived at Auschwitz on a cloudy morning on May 19, 1944. When the boxcar doors were opened, we could see guard dogs, barbed wire, electric fences and high towers with machine guns and SS troops on them. Some prisoners in striped suits tried to help us, saying, "*Raus, Raus*" ("Get out quickly, get out"). People were relieved to be getting out of the boxcars, expecting to get food and water and breathe fresh air. There was no food and water for us, and the air was filled with an awful stench. One prisoner was shouting to cover what the other prisoner was whispering to me: "Give the child to an older woman." I had my niece Judy with me and Mama had the other two, one in her arms and one hanging onto her coat. The prisoner spoke German, but I understood him because at home we spoke Yiddish, which was very similar to German. I didn't do what he said, so he repeated it. I felt that he knew something and was trying to help me, so I gave my niece to Mama. I had always taken care of Judy at home after Sarah's death, intending to raise her myself when I got married. These prisoners tried to save many young mothers and their children from being taken immediately to the gas chamber. They approached one young mother and her four-year-old son and told her what they had told me. In Hungarian, she asked why she should do this, but in the end she gave her child to her mother, who was standing with her. The little boy cried, "I don't want to go with Bubba, I want to go with you!" These were the last words this mother heard from her child.

They made the men go in one line and the women in another, four or five in a row. The horrible smell reminded me of when we burned the last feathers off of chickens after we had plucked them. I didn't know then why they had those high chimneys that always had smoke coming out of them. We were shocked, puzzled and fearful. What was going on here? Why were we brought here? Where would we be working? They told us that they wanted us to work when they forced us out of our homes. While I was walking from the train to the gate I remembered the stories we had heard over the past few years about what was happening to Jews in Poland, Austria and Czechoslovakia while we were still safe in our home. The Poles had been suffering since 1939.

We stopped at the gate, where there was an officer with a little wand in his hand. This was the Angel of Death, Doctor Mengele. By pointing the wand, without saying a word, he indicated which direction each person was to go. In this way, he decided who would live and who would die.

Before we got to that point Mama said to me,

"I'd rather they shoot you than touch you." Those were her last words to me. I have wondered many times why my mother would say such a thing. I didn't know then what she meant. We had no choice about whether we were going to be raped or not. We had no chance to say, "You better shoot me, don't rape me." Was it better in her mind that I die rather than be raped? It bothered me for the longest time that my mother would wish me dead rather than be "unclean." I would want my daughter alive, no matter what, so she could tell people what had happened in that place. I thank God that I was not raped.

At the gate my younger sister and I were sent to the right with other young women, while my two brothers and my brother-in-law went to the left with my father. My older brother Martin was a small person who had been born with one leg shorter than the other. It wasn't noticeable when he walked because he had orthopedic shoes. But when they stripped him nude they could tell, and I assume that he was sent immediately to the gas chamber. My sister-in-law and her baby went in another direction, along with my mother and her three grandchildren.

As our group of young women approached the first buildings we had to take our clothes off. We were stripped naked outside, in the open, with a half dozen SS officers looking at our bodies. There was still a red scar from my appendix operation in February so when I took off my clothes I hung them on my arm, covering the scar. I don't know why I did this, as most of the other girls held their clothes in front of them, trying to cover themselves. However, this action saved my life, as they only wanted strong, physically fit workers, and I would probably have been sent to the gas chambers if they had seen the scar.

Those of us who passed this selection process were sent to the bathhouse, a very large room with signs on the walls in Hungarian, Romanian, Yiddish, Greek and Polish: "Cleanliness keeps you alive. One louse can kill you." We were told to hang our clothes on the hooks on the walls and put our shoes on the floor, neatly tied together. We expected to retrieve them after having a shower, but we never saw our clothes again.

They cut our hair, shaved us everywhere and gave each of us a long gray dress, wooden shoes that had been dipped in disinfectant, and a gray blanket. As we were going through the building, a glass wall separated us from the men, and I saw my father nude for the first time in my life. That was also the last time I saw my father.

We lived in Lagar A, a dark barrack, which had bunk-like cubicles where we were supposed to sit and sleep. However, since there were eight of us in each cubicle, we could not lie down. We had to sit and sleep in a fetal position. There was no toilet in the barrack, just a small a hole in the cement floor at the end of the room and a bucket where we could pee. Every night we could hear black trucks moving around the camp collecting prisoners — 2000 per night — and taking them to the gas chambers. We lived in constant fear that one night they would come for us.

Four *stubava*, female prisoners taken years earlier from Austria, Poland and Czechoslovakia, supervised each barrack. They were angry that we had done nothing to help them when they were being taken prisoners, and sometimes they couldn't help taking this anger out on us. I thought they were absolutely right to feel that way.

We had seen many older people and children being taken into the bathhouse, and we still hadn't seen any of them come out. We imagined there was a back door and that was the reason we hadn't seen them come out. When we asked the *stubava* about this, one of them said, "Are you crazy? You'll never see your mothers, fathers, sisters or grandparents again." She pointed to the high chimneys, "You see the smoke and flames? That's where they went. That's the only way out of here."

Every day we got a cup of soup and a piece of dark bread. The bread tasted like sawdust, probably because that's what was in it. Often I was so numb with fear that I could not tell whether I was hungry or not. One day another prisoner and I were chosen to go to the kitchen with a *stubava* to bring back the soup. On the way we had to pass what appeared to be a family camp, and the other prisoner and I wanted to talk through the barbed wire to the people in there to see if we could get any information about our families. The *stubava* immediately stopped us from doing this, saying, "Do you want to go to the crematorium? We are already on the way there; it's not too far from the kitchen. In Auschwitz you don't speak to anyone and you don't cry or you're dead." They told us that these families behind the barbed wire were being used by Dr. Mengele for medical experiments and would later be exterminated.

Each step we took on the way to and from the soup kitchen was filled with fear. We could see flames and smoke in the near distance. As we passed the crematorium area, there were dead bodies everywhere. There was always that sickening smell in the air and we could hear people screaming. At the time, we didn't know why they were screaming, but we found out later that they were being herded into the "bathhouses" to be executed. Once the people were jammed in and the doors were closed the chemical Zyclon B, mixed with other chemicals to produce cyanide gas, was pumped out of the showerheads instead of water. This gas was heavy and settled near the floor at first, then worked its way up to the ceiling. This meant that everybody did not die at the same time. The young, the old and the sick were always closest to the floor. People gasping for air climbed on top of other people and bodies, and the pile got higher and higher. When the bathhouse doors were opened children were found with their heads crushed and their arms distended and dislocated. Sometimes those people nearest to the roof were able to survive, but they were shot as soon as they were found.

Did Mama watch her little grandchildren die or did she die before they did? Did these little kids have to watch or were they gassed first? Did they die quickly?

8.

SLAVE LABOUR

My youngest sister, Fradel, was with me all along, as we fought to survive our horrific journey together. I had a lot of fear for her, but also for me, as I didn't want to lose her and be left all alone. One day when we were lining up to be tattooed on the arm, a delegation of six well-dressed businessmen with high black hats arrived to look us over. Two thousand young people were chosen to go to work and Fradel and I were among them.

Before we got on the trains to go to the new location, we were taken to a bathhouse to get cleaned up. We saw a train standing on the tracks and prisoners were being thrown like sacks of potatoes straight from the train onto trucks. Woman, children and old people were thrown alive on top of each other and taken directly to the gas chambers. I can still see an old man with a white beard standing up in the truck with his arms and face raised toward heaven calling out to God, *"Shami Israel, Shami Israel "* (O hear yea, O hear yea). This scene is burned into my memory because he looked so much like my grandfather.

It was a great relief, of course, to be getting away from Auschwitz with its smell of flesh, fire pits, gas chambers, black trucks, surprise soup, and intense fear. We were so numb from shock and fear we didn't know where we were going. I remember little of the journey. Perhaps I choose not to remember.

They took us to Düsseldorf where there were oil fields. We unloaded bricks from freight ships and cleaned up rubbish from the bombing. We lived in tents and slept on the ground with only one blanket each. The people from the docks who had paid the SS for our labor couldn't believe that the SS had made us look so ugly: hairless, wearing long gray dresses, with clogs on our feet. The owners gave us food, perhaps a little more than we would have had in Auschwitz because they wanted us to have enough strength to work hard.

One day I almost got separated from my sister, which would have been unbearable at that time. A delegation of well-dressed businessmen from the Krupp munitions company chose 520 girls to go to Essen to make ammunition. Fradel was chosen and as she went on the other side of the fence the SS officer sent me back. But one of the Germans from the Krupp manufacturers said, "No, no, that's the best one of them." My sister and I and the other chosen women travelled on broken-down, windowless streetcars.

We arrived at Essen, at a camp where Italian soldiers had been imprisoned. Every day we marched back and forth between the camp and the Krupp factory. The Allies were bombing frequently now and we were afraid of being injured or killed. They levelled the city of Essen, leaving nothing but rubbish. On October 23, 1944, the Allies dropped phosphate bombs on our camp while we were away working, and we came back from the factory to find our barracks had been levelled. We were petrified that the Germans would shoot us on the spot because they had nowhere to put us. Maybe they didn't shoot us because the Krupp company paid them a lot of money for our work at the factory. All the buildings in the camp made of wood had burned to the ground, but the kitchen had a cement floor, and its basement had survived. So that became our home — 520 of us below ground with no windows, no heat and no water. The floor was covered with straw, but condensation dripping from the cement ceiling five feet above us, combined with our urine, caused the straw to rot. There were outdoor privies but we often used the straw floor for bathroom purposes, as it was cold outside and we were afraid of the German soldiers. The smell was sickening. It was a good place for lice to multiply, and they were carriers of typhoid fever. Our gray blankets were wet most of the time. For six months we lived in that basement, in nauseating and unspeakable conditions. During the winter months we were cold, wet and covered with lice.

While we were in Auschwitz they had given us something in our food to stop the women from menstruating. When I got to this camp in Düsseldorf,

I started to menstruate and I was frightened out of my mind. I didn't know what was happening or what I was going to do, so I talked to the woman who was sort of our leader and she gave me some pieces of rags. I didn't know whether other girls had experienced the same thing or whether I was the only one. I was very frightened because there was so much I did not know.

Sometimes I was put to work pushing a wheelbarrow full of rubbish, and the guards outside kept telling me to fill it even more. They wanted us to get the big bomb craters filled up as quickly as possible. The manufacturers paid the SS for our labour so they wanted to get as much work out of us as possible. I have a bad back today from shovelling and pushing the overloaded wheelbarrow, trying to do the work of two people. I don't know how I managed to push those heavy wheelbarrows without ripping my appendix scar open.

One foreman, a German civilian named Johann, took me up some stairs to teach me how to operate a crane that ran 75 feet above the floor. The crane had a double claw that moved bundles of long steel pipes from one side of the factory to the other. Needless to say, I was petrified, as I had no way of knowing how to operate such a machine. We hadn't been trained at home for that kind of work. However, Johann showed me what to do. My sister was sweeping on the main floor under Johann's supervision, so I felt she was safe. He knew my fears for my baby sister and he let her hide in his little sheet metal office in the corner. When I saw somebody coming, Fradel had to pretend she was holding a shovel or a broom. Another foreman might have had me shot for hiding my sister.

I was always worried about dropping those pipes on the German people who were working below. Obviously they would think I had done it on purpose and I would be shot. One day one of the big bosses, one of those guys with the high hat and hard black boots, came up to check on me operating the crane. I was frightened because I was aware that young women were being raped at that time. I feared he was going to rape me right in that little cabin because he looked me up and down and the look on his face frightened me. I thank God that nothing happened that day. Johann used to come up to the crane frequently, but I never feared him. He was very friendly and gave me a little extra food, which I shared with the other girls. Sometimes Johann dropped carrots, apples and biscuits from the crane, giving us a little extra nourishment.

When two young girls at the camp were sick I asked Johann if he could give me aspirin for them and he brought me some the next day. The girls were very grateful and wanted to give me their four-ounce ration of bread. I couldn't take food from sick children who needed all their energy to get well. The two girls died later. They did not die of starvation, because the Krupp factory supervisors fed us a bit more than we would have got in Auschwitz or any of the other camps. The girls just weren't able to hang on emotionally or spiritually. We were too afraid to show any emotion for the deaths of these girls, because any show of emotion ensured death.

Another time Johann gave me some money and sent me to the canteen in the factory to buy soft drinks for him and me. The bombing in October had destroyed everything in the camp and we didn't have water there, so we were allowed to take tea from the factory back to the camp. As we were marching on the road to the camp the bottle of pop fell out of my rag bag and I thought, *Oh, my God, now I'm going to be shot.* One of the female SS guards bent down, picked up the bottle and gave it back to me, thinking it was tea.

Later on, six of us were sent to work on a flat section of the roof, climbing up a 60-foot ladder to get there. We had to go down this ladder every time we needed to go to the bathroom. I was always terrified of falling. While we were there we repaired skylight windows with putty and used heavy tar to patch the holes caused by explosions.

The Allies were getting closer every day and the air raids were frequent and more severe. They had begun the daylight bombing of Essen. When our camp was hit we were frightened, but we prayed for liberation and were glad they were not far away. Sometimes they bombed and strafed when we were marching to or from the camp. We had to lie down on the road, with only our blankets to cover us, as if the blankets would save us from the bombs that were landing everywhere. These fears were so strong that after awhile my feelings became numb.

In the factory there was a big room with high ceilings where we used to go when the bombs were falling, even though it protected us only from the change in air pressure when the bombs exploded. The Germans wouldn't allow us to go to the shelter under the factory. One morning when we arrived at work that room wasn't there anymore. A bomb had hit it directly and levelled it. It seems we were meant to be saved.

When bombing started while we were at the camp, the Germans would go underground in the coal mine across the road from us while we hid in long, grass-covered bunkers shaped like half moons. Many of the women cried and prayed as we hid in the bunkers. I tried to reassure them that we would be all right, that we would survive. One girl named Bella was convinced that we were all going to die. I kept telling her that we would survive, repeating, "You must have faith. We will be all right, we will survive." I found it was difficult to persuade the young people to think positively even for a short time.

Originally the 520 women shared four bunkers, but 156 Ukrainians arrived and took over the one next to our camp for themselves. They were families — mothers, fathers and children — who came to work voluntarily in Germany. One night, the bombing started and being creatures of habit we ran for all four of the bunkers. The Ukrainians wouldn't allow any Jewish prisoners to enter their bunker because of their strong anti-Semitic feelings, so the 520 of us crammed into the remaining three. We could hear the airplanes above us and the bombs falling. We didn't fear the bombs we heard — it's the one you don't hear that kills you. We also felt the air pressure change when they exploded. It was horrendous. After the air raid ended the SS came from their coalmine bunker and moved us back to our basement living quarters.

The next morning we lined up outside as we did every morning, to be counted to be sure no one had escaped. We saw that the bunker that the Ukrainian people had been in was gone. One of the bombs had hit it and all we had felt at the time was a change in air pressure. Every one of those 156 people, men, women and children had been wiped out, right in the bunker. The SS and other Germans who had gone across to the coal mine said, "From here on in we'll go where the *Yuden* (Jews) go." They were so amazed that this tragedy happened to the Ukrainian families, yet the Jews were unhurt. I felt bad in spite of the fact that the Ukrainians would not share and let us in during the bombing. As it turned out they had done us a big favour. However, they were still human beings in spite of the fact that they hated us. I especially felt bad about the children because they were still innocent of the racist attitudes and anti-Semitic behaviour of their parents.

One day Johann said, "I want to hide you and your sister. Stay here in the factory the next time there's an air raid. When the Germans go to the bunker I'll hide you and your sister." Being young and naive, I said to him, "I don't want to do that. I want to stay with the rest. Whatever happens to them will happen to me." Maybe I was a fatalist. A few days later, as we were lined up to be counted after an air raid, two girls were missing. They counted us over and over again, but I knew right away who had hidden them. We had to stand in rows for several hours while the SS searched for them with dogs. We were very frightened because we knew that the SS often punished the whole camp when there was an escape. Sometimes they would shoot every tenth prisoner and other times they would shoot everyone in the camp. I think we were spared these punishments by the sacrifice of one woman — the woman in white.

One night I had to get out of the basement because I could not bring myself to pee on the straw. There was no light outside so I found my way by crawling through the snow and rubbish. I saw two people by the wall, a blonde woman wearing a white pantsuit and the SS commander of the camp. The woman was in her late 20s, a little bit older than I was, and she came from Sziget, the same town where my grandfather had lived. I could only see her back, as she was kneeling in front of him. He was a shrimp and couldn't have been more than five-feet tall. When I saw what they were doing I was petrified because I had never seen anything like that ever before — sex and lovemaking were never discussed in a Hasidic family — and I was afraid of being seen. She would have had no choice anyway. It was either sex or death, so she was wise to do what the SS commander wanted her to do. I remembered Mama saying to me at the gates of Auschwitz: "Better they shoot you than touch you." In her mind it would be better for me to die than have somebody use me sexually. I disagree with that philosophy. I would have done the same thing as the woman in white. I believe this woman's sacrifice saved us from being shot that morning. I saw her again in Bergen-Belsen but I don't know what happened to her after that.

I remembered my father telling us that thousands of young women had been taken from Austria and Czechoslovakia and trucked to the front lines to be used by the soldiers. When the troops moved on the women were murdered and left in the fields. Perhaps that explains my mother's remark at the gate of Auschwitz.

We had a different foreman, a German civilian named Tony, supervising us up on the roof and I used to talk to him to distract him while the girls warmed their hands over a little round metal drum where we burned rubbish, coal, and pieces of wood. He told me he was aware of what I was doing, but he kept talking to me anyway. He was very worried that if the Russians came they would rape his 15-year old daughter. I asked him why the Russians should treat the Germans any differently than the Germans were treating us. He told me that the Germans would kill us before the war was over, whether they won or lost. He was right.

When the Allied troops were two hours away from one camp, the SS filled buildings with prisoners and set the buildings on fire. Adolph Eichmann had ordered that if the Allies got close to the camps prisoners were to be taken on death marches — forced to walk until they died. Five thousand prisoners from one camp were taken on a death march, 20,000 from another camp and 25,000 from another. In the last few months of the Russian advance on Auschwitz, the fire pits, the gas chambers and the crematoria were working overtime on Eichmann's orders, killing and cremating 12,000 people a day. There was no selection process anymore because there was only one objective: Kill all the survivors.

On one death march the SS stopped at a farmer's field where there were a number of large barns. One of the prisoners asked the SS to let them go because the Allies were so close. The SS soldier said, "Wait, I'll be back." When he came back he had about 50 *Hitler Yungan* (Hitler Youth) with him. These youths forced the prisoners into the barns and set the barns on fire. Those who tried to escape the burning barns were shot as they emerged. However, a few people did manage to escape, and I met one of these escapees in Sweden, a Hungarian Jew named Laci. His face had been burned during the barn fire and he died some time later of facial cancer.

The foreman on the roof expressed his hatred for Jews and kept telling me that the Germans would kill all the Jews one way or another. I told him, ""That's not possible. You can't wipe out every Jew." He did not respond to my remark and I became fearful of him reporting me to the SS guards who were keeping warm downstairs. He could have had me shot on the spot. But he didn't. Could it be because he was a civilian? Maybe he had some compassion because he realized that if the Russians took over his part of Germany (which they did) he would have to fear for his family. I asked myself why I had risked my life by saying such things. I will never forget that conversation.

After our conversation he allowed me to heat up a pail of water. I went behind a metal wall and pulled my dress off my shoulders to wash my upper body and my hair. I was afraid to undress completely for fear of being seen and raped. It was about minus-5 degrees Celsius at the time, so the water felt heavenly. We had had no water in the camp since October 1944, and it was now late December. We were allowed to take water and tea from the factory back to the camp, but it was usually only a pop bottle of liquid, and it had to last until we returned to the factory in the morning, so I could not use any of it to wash myself. Even though this foreman seemed to agree with what the Nazis were doing, his act of kindness reminded me that there could still be humanity in the midst of all that horror. I learned never to give up hope. Never ever.

I felt fortunate that we had been taken from Auschwitz to Essen. Having Fradel with me helped a great deal, and I worked hard to shelter her from the guards. I think that my fear for my sister and others added strength to my will to survive. I have always been concerned for the welfare of others, even as a child. Had I been thinking only of myself I might not have survived. Also, I was determined not to let the SS defeat me.

9.

BERGEN-BELSEN

In early February 1945 we heard rumours that they were going to move us from Essen because the Russians were getting closer. One of our guards, a Hungarian soldier, was a Schwab, a descendent of Germans who had gone to Hungary and Transylvania before the First World War. He spoke our language with a German dialect. He wasn't as cruel as some of the other guards. I also got the feeling that he was a little bit ashamed of what was going on and how we were being treated.

About the middle of February they took us away by train and we had no idea where we were going. The train ride was horrific, because the train went backward and forward, shunting from one track to another to avoid the bombing that was in progress. We were on the train for quite a few days without food. At night the train would sit still because the bombs were dropping all around us and they couldn't move. One night the Schwab soldier went out into the farm fields and came back with sacks full of sugar beet. There was no water, so we ate the beets, mud and all. Of course, we ate it; we would have eaten anything that anybody gave us.

One day we stopped at a camp, which I believe was Buchenwald. I saw electrical fences, prisoners who looked like skeletons walking around, dead bodies on the ground, and male prisoners wearing odd caps who stared at the train. The SS left our train and entered the camp. The fear of them taking us off this train and putting us in this camp was almost unbearable. When the SS returned to the train we continued our journey. Later that evening the Schwab told us they wouldn't take us in that camp because it was overloaded. I thought it was a miracle that we weren't let into that camp, even though we didn't know where we were going to end up.

When the train finally stopped, we were marched into another concentration camp, Bergen-Belsen. This camp, which was 9 square miles and was built to hold 7,000 soldiers, now held over 50,000 prisoners. One of the SS women who was with us in Essen was crying. I don't know if she was crying for herself or for us because she had got attached to us. In Essen she used to send me to the SS quarters to get her meal in her blue enamel container. Sometimes she would leave some food in the container and I would finish it before returning the container to her quarters.

Gradually the full horror of this camp became apparent. The prisoners were walking skeletons. As we got further into the camp we saw hills of dead bodies and skeletons lying on top of each other, mountains of them. I did not see any chimneys or people being loaded onto trucks directly from the train and taken to the gas chambers as they had done in Auschwitz. It was petrifying. They took us to a barrack where we sat down on the floor. Two other girls from my hometown were in the same barrack with me. One was Iren, the daughter of our neighbour across the street, the one whose house I wasn't supposed to go into because they had modern ideas, a radio, books, and movie magazines. I know she survived because she came to visit me in Sweden. The other girl, Bella, was with us in the bunker in Essen, and I used to give her pep talks to convince her that we would get out of this. But she was sure we were going to be wiped out. I told her that she had to have faith because that would also give her hope.

There were no bunks or anything to lie on. Walking skeletons and human waste filled the barracks. The smell was beyond description. We had not seen anything in previous camps to match this inhuman scene. There was so much death and dying, pain, and suffering completely stripped of human dignity. Some people were not even moving; others were so weak and sick they were lying in their own diarrhea. I don't know how long they'd been there. I guess we were very fortunate that the Krupp manufacturers had rented us as slave labour from the SS, because they gave us a little bit of food which gave us the energy to survive this horrific ordeal. After the shock of seeing our barrack we lined up outside to be counted. There was no water or toilets anywhere. We got a cup of tea and a cup of soup made out of potato peels. I never saw a piece of bread while I was there. I found a tap outside a barrack that would sometimes have water dripping into a round cement basin. It must have been from the Wermacht days. The ground outside was crawling with lice and covered with diarrhea and dead bodies.

One day in March 1945 I was scouting around outside, seeing if I could recognize anyone, when I met Lazar's girlfriend. I hardly recognized her and had to look twice to be sure it was her. She was a walking blonde skeleton. Lazar had been very fond of her and saw her whenever he could sneak away from my parents. I was so shocked I didn't ask what camps she had survived. I asked her if she had seen my brother or anyone from home. She said she had seen Lazar pushing a cart with other prisoners. I was in such a state of shock that I didn't ask her what camp it was. A few days later I went to look for her so I could ask questions but I never saw her again. I imagine she died like so many others, just walking around till they dropped. I am still dealing with the lack of information about my brother's death. I did search in 1946 and 1947 through the Red Cross in Sweden and they could find no information for me. In 1952 I made another search in Canada.

A man who had been our pharmacist in Szatmar asked me if I had seen his wife. He used to be a very handsome man, but I barely recognized him. He was haggard, hairless, and wrapped in a dirty gray blanket. I hadn't seen his wife, nor did I know where she ended up. The group they had selected for forced labour was made up of younger people, and the pharmacist's wife was older. When I last saw the pharmacist he was dragging corpses out of the barracks and throwing them onto the mountains of bodies or into ditches. The SS assassinated men and women and then had prisoners deal with the corpses. The smell of dead and dying people was sickening. A woman who had lived on our street in Szatmar asked me if I had seen her sister, but I couldn't help her either. People in the camp were always asking other prisoners if they had seen their families and loved ones.

I became very itchy and scratched myself to get the lice off me. It was a losing battle, as nobody cleaned up anything. At times I wondered if it was safer in the barrack or outside among the dead bodies. Inside each barrack were about 100 dead, dying, or diseased prisoners. Outside there were several hills of dead bodies and also bodies of people who had just died and had not yet been removed to the piles or the ditches. Before I became ill I took Fradel with me and searched every day for familiar faces — cousins, or neighbours or anyone I had known before we were removed to the camps. I even went to the piles of dead bodies hoping to find someone I recognized. There were often new dead bodies nearby. Once I saw a young face in the pile of bodies. All the other bodies were skeletons but her face was still young and beautiful. I still wonder how she came to be there on that pile, as she was the only one who was not a skeleton. Perhaps she was raped and then shot. I continued to search for familiar faces every day, with no luck.

I lived minute-by-minute and each day became an eternity. As the days went by we became more numb, weak from lack of food and water. In my case, I was lucky because I had people to talk to, our neighbour's daughter and my sister. Two sisters from Sziget, my grandfather's hometown, had arrived at Belsen the same day we had and ended up in the same barrack.

A week before liberation one of them stole some potato peelings from the kitchen and was shot in the leg. I found out later that 67 others had been shot for the same reason. I know the sisters survived because both of them came to see me in Sweden. You had to be very careful of every move you made, every look you gave, so you didn't draw any attention to yourself. Survival is a very strong instinct but you have to be aware of it every minute.

Every night the Allies' artillery shells fell closer and closer and we could see the glow of the fires in the distance. We didn't know what was happening, just that the Allies were getting closer. We were afraid the SS would kill us before the Allies arrived because the foreman on the roof in Essen had said, "The Germans will kill you before the Allies get there. The Germans will kill you if they win; they will kill you if they lose." We didn't know what was going to happen from minute to minute.

I don't think anyone can imagine or understand the shock that witnessing such indescribably horrific

These pictures were taken by an SS officer and were given to Eva by Rude Olsson in Stockholm in 1945.

conditions can have on the mind. I was afraid to lie
down for fear I might not get up, afraid to sit down
because I might be eaten by the lice, afraid to stand
up for fear I'd fall down. If I fell down, who would
look after my sister? I still wonder today how I
survived this shocking display of inhumanity and the
complete denial of all human value. I found out later
there had been cannibalism there and in Auschwitz
too. It is really mind-boggling to think of those
diseased bodies being eaten by dying prisoners, but
it shows how human beings can be dehumanized to
the point where they'll do anything for survival. To
eat human flesh, one must have lost all faith and hope.

Eventually I did fall ill with typhoid. No matter
how sick we were, we were supposed to go outside
to be counted, but there were days I couldn't do it. I
had a high fever and just lay among the dead bodies
on the floor, covered with lice. I had never even heard
of typhus before, so I didn't know what why I was
so sick. Most of the other prisoners had dysentery
(non-stop diarrhea), but I had the opposite problem.
For ten days I couldn't go to the bathroom. Of
course, the body needs food before it can produce
waste, and we were barely getting starvation rations.
Then six days before the Allies arrived the SS shut
the water off completely and took away our food
rations. Perhaps they felt that without food or water
we would all die, and many people did. Many
prisoners were just skin and bones, their eyes bulging
out of their sunken bodies, barely recognizable as
human. They died and fell to the floor or onto the

ground. I feel they died free, at peace, not like prisoners in other camps who were gassed or burned alive in fire pits. The sight of it overpowered the eyes and the mind. At that point I was too sick to care what was happening or think about what the outcome would be. I was so hot with fever that I peed on a rag and put it on my head, hoping it might cool me down. However, we were all suffering from dehydration too, so not much fluid came out of me.

One morning I was too sick to go outside and the girls stood for several hours waiting to be counted. Some of the girls collapsed and were dragged into the barracks. About two hours later the rest of the girls came back in and told me that the SS guards had left and come back with white bands on their arms. They had surrendered to the Allies.

10.

LIBERATION

The Allies arrived on the morning of April 15. That day felt like the first day of my life, the day I was reborn. I lay there and waited for the Allies to come into the barrack. When they did, they looked around, trying to decide how to deal with what they saw. The soldiers put red crosses on the foreheads of those prisoners who were not skeletons, and they were to be taken out first to be disinfected. Those skeletons too weak to stand or walk were treated on the spot and later taken to tents for further treatment. People who were lying in their waste and couldn't move were left till the last.

First they took us to a tent where they disinfected us by washing us with a solution. I suppose they didn't want to take those horrific diseases out of the camps. My whole body was covered in spots, and I found out later at the hospital that it was fleck typhus — typhoid with spots. Fradel was not sick at that point and I was very concerned that they were going to separate us when they took me to the hospital two miles outside the Bergen-Belsen camp boundaries. I cried and I begged the army officers to let her come with me and they did, taking us to the hospital in a military ambulance. The hospital was a converted German training centre for Panzer Tank military operations.

The British captain in charge of the negotiation process to take over the camp questioned the German camp commander, Josef Kramer, as Kramer gave him a tour of the camp. Kramer described the camp prisoners as habitual criminals, felons and homosexuals. Classifying all of the prisoners as criminals and felons was Kramer's way of justifying his criminal, insane treatment of them. During the tour the British captain could hear gunfire close by and realized that the killing was still going on even after the surrender. Kramer was told that if any more prisoners were shot, an equal number of Germans would be shot. The killing stopped.

Many prisoners were so ill and far-gone that they were treated on the spot as best they could be. Those who managed to live were later removed to tent areas as the barracks were burned to the ground to prevent the spread of disease. Fradel and I were lucky to be taken to the hospital. Many thousands of prisoners did not make it out of the camp alive even after liberation. I found out later that Anne Frank died in Bergen-Belsen when I was a prisoner there.

Just as I was getting better, my sister's condition worsened. Fradel caught typhus and was delirious with fever, talking in her sleep at night. She thought she was back at home. One time she said, "It's Friday. You have to go and clean the boys' shoes and get their white shirts out," because the girls usually got the boys' clothes ready for the Sabbath. She really was not doing too well. I was getting better because I had already been quite sick before we were liberated.

I could not bear to see my sister so sick. One day a doctor came in, looked at me, looked at my sister, and left without making a comment. I got out of bed and went after her. I said to her, "You can't let her die." The doctor kept going, so I grabbed her by her white coat and said, "You cannot let her die. She's all I have." The doctor said, "I'll see what I can do." She came back with a needle, gave my sister an injection, and said, "That's really all I can do for her. If it works, she will live, and if it doesn't work, she won't." My sister slept and slept and woke up two or three days later, feeling better. Obviously, that medication helped her, whatever it was. She got better and that helped me.

The other lady in the room was around 40. One day when I felt better I got out of my bed and asked her what was wrong with her. She told me that she was in the Yugoslavian underground and was captured. They put her in solitary confinement in Treblinka, and for punishment they kept her standing on wooden boards with the nails pointing upwards. Her feet were all blue and swollen. We talked about what was happening in the war. She couldn't talk much because she was still in shock, so I said little and listened. During the months I was in the hospital I picked up a lot of information from the staff and other survivors. We all wanted to know who had survived, who had died, and how many more would die.

Every three days or so a British army officer named Frank arrived from the lab to take blood samples. He became friendly with me, perhaps because he liked me or felt sorry for me. Either way, he used to bring me a little bit of extra food because the food we got in the hospital had to be bland because our stomachs wouldn't take anything else. In fact, 13,000 died after liberation because they couldn't tolerate the food or overate until their stomachs exploded, or they were too far-gone to be helped and they passed on. Frank asked Fradel and me to go to a movie when we were feeling better. Frank brought a friend with him. I don't remember what was playing or the name of the town we were in, but I remember the people laughing. When he asked us to go again my sister did not want to go. She had gone the one time but she felt that movies weren't really compatible with her Hasidic beliefs and upbringing.

I went out with Frank a few times and he asked me if I would like to go to England. His wife was dead and he had a nine-year-old boy. I chose not to go to England even though I realized his feelings were honourable.

Then the Red Cross asked if we wanted to go to Sweden or another country, maybe even back home to Hungary. At this point that I began to realize that not only was I physically free, I was also free to make my own decisions about the rest of my life. I could not see myself going back to Hungary or Romania because the regimes in both these countries had helped the Nazis try to exterminate us. They informed the SS where we were hiding, then took the land, homes and personal property of the Jews for themselves. My father, grandfather and great-grandfather were Romanian and my passport is Romanian, but I could not return to Romania because of their collaboration with the Nazis.

In 1941 and 1942 the old Romanian police force, the Iron Guard, slaughtered a lot of Jews. I remember my father talking to my mother about what happened in Bessarabia and Bukovina and the death march of 120,000 Jews in 1941. My second cousin visited near the end of 1942 and talked to my parents about thousands of Jews who were put on trains that went in circles until most of them perished and others were murdered. Thousands of others died of disease and starvation under the Romanian Regime. The Romanian leader, Antonesai, had already signed a treaty with Hitler to collaborate with the SS in 1940. In one instance, Jews were placed in a slaughterhouse with signs reading "Kosher Meat" around their necks. Then they were killed with axes and other weapons. Their houses were burned to the ground and all their personal property was confiscated. At that time the Germans did not occupy Hungary and we still felt relatively safe.

If I returned to Romania, I would never feel safe. I would live in fear of betrayal for the rest of my days, fear that those who had committed genocide

once would do it again. I couldn't understand why
the 350,000 Jews remaining from the original 750,000
before the war chose to stay in Romania. Why did
they not flee the country? Why would they stay and
live with their murderers? Much later I learned that
the government was holding them for ransom.
Thousands of Jews were "sold" to Israel and other
countries for billions of dollars, and I am told that
this ransom program was continued into the 1980s.
For years, the government would not issue passports
to Jews in Romania until $1000 was paid. Why would
I want to go back to Romania?

So I decided that Fradel and I would go to
Sweden. I didn't know much about Sweden, but when
the war started in 1939, I heard my parents talking
about how Sweden, this tiny little country, was going
to remain neutral. We travelled by train from Belsen
to Berlin along with a lot of other refugees, including
orphans whose parents had been killed in the camps.
A nice-looking young man with curly hair was looking
out the same window as me on the train when he
turned and kissed me. I was shocked, because no
one else had ever kissed me before, other than my
parents and my siblings when I was a child. This
was not acceptable to a girl coming from a family
where such things were forbidden. I was so naive I
slapped him across the face. Years later I realized I
was reacting to my childhood "tapes" — an
immediate and automatic response from my
childhood training. After the atrocities and
dehumanization of Bergen-Belsen and Auschwitz I

should have been grateful for any show of affection instead of reacting so negatively. I don't know how the boy felt, only that he stared at me in astonishment. He certainly did not deserve a slap in the face, and if I met him today I would apologize. His action was not acceptable to me then, but today I welcome a hug and a kiss because they give such positive energy. It is not forbidden anymore.

We were given a medical inspection at the dock in Lubeck, Germany, prior to leaving by boat for Sweden. There were no rooms with bunks or beds on the boat so we lay on the floor. The sea was rough going across to Sweden, and we were rolling into each other. The food we got on board was very bland, kind of like Jell-O, but I think it was made out of a rosebud seed. We weren't able to eat much anyway. I heard later that some refugees died after arriving in Sweden because their stomachs couldn't handle food.

11.

SWEDEN

We arrived at the port city of Helsenborg and were taken by train to a quarantine area in Malmö, near the Danish border. We were kept there under observation for three weeks to be sure we weren't bringing any diseases into the country. They gave us some regular clothes (not gray dresses!) and our hair had started to grow back in, so we began to look more like human beings. My hair was always very curly. We used to look out the window and watch the people go by. One day I received a package from Jösta, a man who had seen me in the window as he walked by on the street. He sent me a hand mirror, lipstick, hairbrush, pad of paper, and a pencil, all in a cardboard box wrapped in paper with a pink bow and ribbon. They brought the box in to me and he waited outside on the street until I had received his parcel. I couldn't understand why he had picked me to receive the gift. I don't know what he was expecting. Were we that unusual to the Swedish people? They had not been in the war or affected by the Holocaust, and Jews who lived in Sweden had not been touched in any way. In fact, many Jewish people were smuggled out of Denmark into Sweden in 1943.

One day Jösta got permission to take me out of this place two or three days before our quarantine was up. He took me to an area near a big body of water, and then to dinner with a Swedish family. I didn't speak a word of Swedish, but I could communicate a few words in German because it is similar to Yiddish in many ways. This was such a lovely, human, social experience after that of the camps. The Swedish people were so different and treated me very nicely. There were also some young people there who must have been their children or relatives visiting the summer home by the water. The dinner table was beautifully set, very different from that in a Hasidic home. They had these open-face sandwiches, a smorgasbord as it is called. I didn't know how you should eat these sandwiches, as I had never seen one before. At home we picked up a piece of bread and if we had something to put on it we just put it on and ate it. But I was intelligent enough to know what not to do, so I waited to see what the other people did with the slice of bread with all the goodies on top. First they put it on their plate, then they used their forks and knives to cut and eat it. After dinner he took me back to where I was staying. I never saw him again.

Finally the day came that we were well and certified to be in good health. They took us to a summer resort run by Jewish people beside a big body of water near Gustusburg. It was a beautiful place with a gorgeous dining room overlooking the water. I still remember the beautiful formal gardens at the resort that were looked after by gardeners. Everybody had chores to do, like peeling potatoes and vegetables. I was chosen to set the tables and see that the tables were all properly done according to Swedish tradition because the Swedish people are very fussy. We stayed there all that summer.

My friend Berta and I got a three-day pass to go to Stockholm. Fradel didn't go because she felt more comfortable staying with the other religious girls. Berta and I stayed at a hostel in a big, old house, where many other refugees stayed as well. The hostel provided food and we were supposed to go to bed early. After dinner, instead of settling in for the night, we snuck out through the gate and promptly got lost riding a streetcar. The lights of the city were fascinating and we saw a fire engine that wasn't horse-drawn! Some time later we asked the conductor to read the piece of paper given to us when we had arrived and he sent us in the right direction to return to our hostel. We knew it was late and we were frightened and worried. When we arrived at the hostel the courtyard gate was locked, but we found an open window and crawled safely into the dark building. I slid into a bunk bed and fell asleep. Sometime later I was awakened by a hand on my shoulder and a short man with a round face and black hair saying in Yiddish, "You can't sleep here; this is my bed." I was so tired I couldn't remember where my bed was. The next morning we were gently reprimanded, "This conduct is just not acceptable." However, freedom was a new experience for us and we'd have to get used to it again. Three days later we returned to the resort and stayed there until it closed for the season.

Sometimes I found myself afraid of this new freedom. Each one of us had to face a new journey and the fear of not knowing what the journey would be like or where it would take me was frightening. I had never known this kind of fear before. At home my environment was controlled and secure. While I was in the camps my life was controlled and insecure while I fought for survival. As I left the resort I had none of these controls and plenty of insecurity. I know now my insecurity was the result of my lack of education, my ignorance of social differences and customs, and my fear of failure. Gradually I came to realize that I would have to make the most of what lay ahead of me. I also realized I must not lose the faith that got me through all those atrocities in the camps.

Berta and I were always exploring. We'd go to a little grocery shop and we buy a loaf of French bread, a piece of kolbassa and some pickles. I can still see us on a gorgeous, sunny day sitting on the stone curbs by the road eating like two kids. We were so excited to be free, able to bite into this meat and eat it, we didn't care that it wasn't kosher. It is hard to describe the feeling of freedom that gave us, just the simple freedom to choose.

But we couldn't stay at the resort forever. The time came for each of us to move on in different directions. My sister decided to go to a Jewish refugee camp in Fairnabrook, which provided schooling for young people. Quite a few of us girls decided to go to work in the porcelain factory in Gustavsberg, which was the next village over from where we were staying.

Fradel didn't approve of me working on the Sabbath and she began to withdraw from me. During our time at the resort she had never given me a chance to sit down to discuss our recent tribulations or our future. We had never talked about our brothers or sisters or other members of our family at any time, even in the camps. I think her actions were an attempt to become my father and control and manipulate my life as she had tried to do as a child. That attempt failed. Her condemnation didn't bother me because I wanted to work. I thought working on the Sabbath was okay because in Sweden most people worked six days a week. My feeling at that point was: "When in Rome do as the Romans do."

Our employers gave us housing and we didn't have to pay rent until we were on our feet and able to do so. The building where we were housed was like a dormitory and was located a little bit out of the village, so we had to cycle or walk to work at the factory. There was a central bathroom, a central wash house and showers, and all the necessary facilities. Berta and I shared a lovely room with two beds, a desk and a dresser.

12.

RUDE

In October there was a dance in the village and some of the girls decided to go and see what it was all about. Everybody was staring at us, the refugees. Our clothes weren't exactly the most elegant. We were dressed in a kind of sporty style, wearing skirts and blouses or whatever clothes they had given us. A young Swedish man named Rude asked me to dance. I wasn't a very good dancer, because when I was growing up, Hasidic girls didn't dance with boys. If we danced at a wedding or any other *simcha* (special occasion), we would dance with girls, so I was very nervous. However, I got my rhythm back and it felt nice to be dancing. Rude kept coming back and asking me to dance. At one point, he saw a girl come into the hall and he went and spoke to her. I didn't know who she was, but she was very well dressed and beautiful, with gorgeous long hair and white teeth. I couldn't speak Swedish so I couldn't ask him what that was all about. It wasn't that important to me at that time because I wasn't looking for a boyfriend. Later he told me the girl at the door had become his ex-girlfriend that night.

That winter I saw Rude only once a week

because he was going to Stockholm's Technical Institute for engineering and had a lot of studying to do. There wasn't really anything transpiring between us then, but it was very nice to have him as a friend. Being with Rude helped me pick up more of the Swedish language, which lessened my feeling of being isolated. I knew that I had to learn the language if I wanted to be able to live on my own and carry on a normal daily life. Sometimes my poor Swedish created humorous situations. At a grocery store I wanted to buy some eggs but I didn't know the Swedish word for eggs, so I imitated a chicken and pointed to my rear. The guy in the store laughed and knew what I wanted. Getting onions or garlic wasn't as easy. However, within six months I spoke Swedish well enough to get by and it also made my work easier. I rejoiced in this feeling of freedom, knowing enough of the language to be able to walk down the street on my own.

Rude invited me to spend Wednesday evenings with him while he studied at his family's home. At first I felt very uncomfortable because of my lack of education. During one of our conversations I asked him why he didn't have a well-educated Swedish girlfriend, and he replied, "You have more in your head than 30 Swedish girls put together." He made me realize that I had inner qualities and spiritual values, and I began to feel less uncomfortable within myself. He had enough insight to see beyond education and appearance. Our relationship grew from this point on.

While Rude studied, I embroidered a tablecloth. When he was finished he would walk me back to my apartment, which was in a dormitory in a wooded area. Our relationship became affectionate and I appreciated his patience. Perhaps he understood that my experiences in the camps had had a negative effect on my sexual feelings. However, he could not know that it went much deeper than that. In my home none of us saw each other half undressed, let alone naked. Sex was never discussed or referred to; sexuality was completely denied. It didn't exist until seven days before marriage. The unspoken message was that you should ignore your own body unless you cut yourself and were bleeding. I was free of the camps but not of the childhood training I had received. I felt very inadequate and unsure of myself in social situations.

One Sunday afternoon in late October1945 Rude, Berta, Irene, and I were sitting on a bed talking about Auschwitz. Irene was telling us about her escape from the black truck that made runs after dark every night picking prisoners from the barracks, although never from mine. One night the black truck stopped at Irene's barrack and placed her and 20 others inside. When they stopped at the next barrack she managed to escape. The rest of the girls were taken to the gas chamber. The black truck made this trip every night, adding even more to our fear of not surviving. We also talked about our fear on the nights when the Gestapo officers would come to the barrack to use the four female *stubavas*. The soldiers had been drinking and we didn't know whether they would go crazy and come to our side of the barrack and rape us. All three of us had different stories of survival. It was not easy to talk about it; perhaps it was too soon. Rude had difficulty with the language, so he listened and I explained later.

I decided that I needed privacy and moved out on my own. After freedom, I treasure privacy most and put a high value on it. I had very little privacy when I was a child at home; then the Nazis took it away completely. In Auschwitz they violated our privacy when they stripped us naked in front of strangers who looked us up and down. All we had left was what was in our souls and they couldn't strip us of that. Rude was very pleased with my decision to get my own place. He felt it was a strong step forward and would make it easier for our courtship to develop. As an apartment-warming gift he bought me a beautiful pair of pale blue silk slippers with white fur pom-poms and tiny heels, just like the movie stars wore in those days.

One day after I got home from work, I decided to have a shower, so I undressed and put on my royal blue bathrobe. I had left my apartment door ajar and when I returned to my apartment Rude was standing there. He had found the door open and when I did not answer he had walked in. He untied the belt of my bathrobe and lifted me onto the bed standing up. I can still see the look on his face as he exposed my body. I was absolutely shocked when he told me I had a beautiful body and should be proud of it.

No, nothing happened that time. We had a lot to discuss before anything did happen. My greatest fear was that if I had sex outside of marriage Rude would think I was a "bad woman" and would leave me. He had great difficulty understanding that my fear of sexual matters stemmed from my childhood training by my family. I couldn't tell him that one night when I was 15 I was sleeping in a bed beside my mother when my father returned from a trip, came into the room and proceeded to have sex with my mother. I lay there awake, confused and frightened, not knowing what was happening, as we had been given no sex education at all. Two of the other children were sleeping in another bed in the same room. I still wonder how my parents could have been so insensitive to the fact that children were in the room and might hear and see them.

As a Swede, Rude could see nothing wrong with two people loving each other and making love. Sometime later, before we became intimate, I was visiting his home on a cold winter night and his mother suggested I stay overnight. I accepted and she made up the sofa bed for two. Rude quietly said to his mom, "Eva and I have yet to sleep together." Rude taught me to open my mind to a new and better way of living. He taught me that it was okay to express myself sexually and to feel good about and love my body. Of course, that can only happen when you begin to love yourself. My experiences in the camps had shut down all possibility of these feelings in me, but Rude's love for me helped to open them up again.

Through his caring, tender, loving presence I began to love myself and allow myself to experience what I had never dreamed was possible. When two people are spiritually well matched, nothing else matters.

I came to love Rude, and when he asked me to marry him, I accepted. We had a three-year engagement during which I saw how caring and humane he was. He wanted us to get married and go to live in Israel so I could be near my sister Fradel. Little did he know what my sister was like. He had a hard time believing that people could live that way and ostracize those people who didn't live their way. When people asked me how could I marry someone out of my faith I always said, "I married a human being, not a religion." I don't believe I married out of my faith. My husband and I had different religious backgrounds, but we both had faith in God and a strong belief in humanity, with tolerance for others. I chose to marry Rude without any consideration of his religion. It doesn't matter who you marry as long as you live the life you were put on earth to live.

Why would I not want to marry a Swede? They took a lot of Jewish people in during the war. The Germans occupied Denmark in 1940 and when they wanted to take the Jews to the death camps in 1943, the Danes smuggled the Jews into Sweden. The Swedes took all those Jews from Denmark with open arms. So if I loved a Swedish or Danish man and he wanted to marry me, why would I say no to him? How could I be prejudiced against Swedes and Danes when they showed only respect and tolerance for me, not prejudice? This demonstration of brotherly love and compassion had a big effect on my life. I could not resent people who had been kind and sheltered so many Jews from the Nazis, just because they had different religious beliefs. I respect and admire these people, as they set a good example for the rest of the world.

When I was living in Sweden and about to be married, something strange happened. I was told that to get a marriage licence I needed to provide the Swedish marriage bureau with a birth certificate. Rude asked a friend who was a detective for advice. He suggested that the only way I could get a licence was if I declared myself stateless. In 1949, shortly after we were married, I received a letter from the Romanian Consulate asking me to return to Romania because the country needed me and would pay my fare. My husband was furious, but I was frightened. I wondered how they had found me and how they knew I had changed my citizenship. Why would they want one more insignificant young Jewish woman to return to Romania? I was fully aware of the atrocities that had occurred in Hungary and Romania. I was not aware then that the Romanian government was selling Jews for ransom money. To my knowledge none of the other women received a request to go home. Was it possible that the Romanian government saw me as a ransom prospect or did they object to my giving up my citizenship? I will never know. This incident discouraged me from ever returning to Romania to search for relatives. In July 1949 I became a Swedish citizen and this gave me a sense of security. Being a Swedish citizen would protect me from the Romanian government. It is my hope that Romanian Jews have found acceptance and peace wherever they are.

In 1949 Rude and I went to the Jewish organization for refugees in Stockholm, because we wanted to get married. Among the refugees there were some very modern rabbis who were qualified to marry people. There was no concern that Rude was a Gentile, but the man we spoke to suggested that if we wanted to get married right away we should go to the city hall and have a civil ceremony. We took his advice. On Saturday, July 9, 1949 Rude and I took the bus into Stockholm. First we had lunch with his Aunt Hilda and her husband. Then Aunt Hilda took me to a salon for brides, where one of the ladies did my hair and fitted me for a white dress and a short veil. Hilda's husband brought Rude to the salon with a bouquet of red and white carnations. It's been said all brides look beautiful and that certainly applied in my case. When we arrived at the Stockholm city hall at three o'clock, Rude's parents, Tura and Gunner, were waiting for us. After a brief ceremony we returned to Aunt Hilda's home for coffee and refreshments.

A short time later we left for a stately hotel where a reception dinner and dance for 50 people had been arranged. The refugee girls I worked with were all invited, and some of Rude's relatives also attended. The dinner was delicious and my father-in-law supplied the table with imported French cognac. The hotel gardens were ideal for taking wedding pictures. We spent our honeymoon at Rude's grandparents' home in a small village in northern Sweden. I certainly have no regrets. The years I was married to Rude were the best 19 years of my adult life.

After Rude and I were married I asked to work half days and they allowed me to do that, as only married women were allowed to work half days. Freedom meant more to me than money. I would go in at six o'clock in the morning and get home at one o'clock in the afternoon. I made good money and I didn't need a lot of material things. Later I transferred to a different department and learned how to paint china cups, plates, saucers, vases, and other beautiful ornamental items.

One day the foreman told me that my work wasn't very good. He said that the gold and green lines I made on the plates and cup handles weren't quite neat enough. I had been asked to do the job faster, and I told the foreman that if he wanted me to increase production I could only do it the way I was doing it. If he wanted me to do a perfect job then I would have to work more slowly, producing fewer pieces. That didn't go over very well with him.

I decided I'd had enough of his complaining and gave him my resignation. The union steward came to see me and asked why I was quitting. I didn't understand what unions were. I had never even heard of unions because I had never worked in a factory other than as forced labour. The steward said the company would give me a raise if I would stay. I said, "No, I won't stay but you can do something for me. You can give that raise to my comrades, the other refugee girls working in the factory. "

A few days after handing in my resignation, I looked for a job in the newspaper. At that time I could already read a little bit of Swedish and I saw an advertisement for a job in a Stockholm candle factory called Liljea Holms that made large candles for churches. I thought I might give it a try, so I called them and was told to come for an interview. I never even told Rude anything about it until I got the job, and he was very surprised that I had been so independent. Rude's kind and generous nature ensured that taking the job wouldn't cause any problems for us. The only difference was that I had to get up earlier and take the bus to Stockholm every morning and back home in the late afternoon, but this worked out very well. I was in a department all by myself, thrilled to be my own boss at last! It was a very nice feeling to be considered dependable and given responsibility. My job was drilling the bottoms of the candles to fit the different shapes of the pegs on the candleholders. When Sweden's King Gustav died in 1950, the demand for candles for all the churches was overwhelming. I was very successful at my work and overwhelmed by the pay and treatment I received at the factory. About this time Rude graduated from the Stockholm Technical Institute. He had a very good position in Gustavsberg designing parts for Electrolux mini-bar refrigerators.

We got a second-floor apartment in a new building in Gustavsberg. Considering the places I had lived in so far in my life, I thought it was just gorgeous! The village was surrounded by woods and it was beautiful and peaceful. We were very happy. My Hungarian friend, Edith, lived beside us with her Swedish boyfriend, Alf, and we used to see each other a lot. She was very modern and had been well educated before the war. It was good to have friends around me. The four of us would go to the Jewish social organization in Stockholm for parties and dances. There was never any question of Rude or Alf being accepted in the group.

My husband bought me the first bicycle I had ever had. Another day when I came home from work there was a beautiful pair of red skis leaning against the wall in the foyer. He had bought them and brought them home on his lunch hour. He taught me to cross-country ski in the nearby woods.

These gifts wouldn't sound like much to children today because they get a lot of toys, bicycles, skis, dolls, and games at Christmas and on their birthdays. They take it for granted that this abundance of gifts is available at all times. But being given gifts such as the bicycle and the skis overwhelmed me and flooded me with memories. Birthdays were never celebrated in Hasidic households, so no gifts were given, even by those who could afford to give them. When relatives visited they did not bring gifts or surprises for the children. When I was a little girl the only doll I had was made out of a piece of firewood. I used to take a piece of rag and make a face by sewing eyes, a mouth and a nose on it. I never had a little shovel or a pail to play in the sand. The big toy store in the town square had two glass display cases filled with bicycles, toys, dolls, teddy bears, gorgeous beach balls, buckets, shovels, and many more wonderful things for children. But none of this was for me. I could only stand and stare at them.

Today's children seem to have so much more than I did as a child, yet I wonder if they have more negative things in their lives than I did. I hope they can find the positives too, in order to balance their lives. My husband helped me to balance my life. He showed me different ways of looking at life by sharing with me his knowledge of a way of living different from that which I had experienced or observed. His concern for my emotional and physical well being was obvious. That's the kind of person he was, always giving me nice surprises and caring about me, asking what I would like.

The Korean War was going on then and I was very frightened. I didn't want to go through another war. The Russians were right beside us in Finland and that scared me. I was worried about what would happen if there was another war. Although I did have a caring husband who was very supportive, I still feared having to go through the horrors I had endured so recently and being left alone again. I knew that this fear was a carry-over in my mind from the earlier atrocities, but I still had to work hard to try and put it behind me. I realized later that the lives of survivors can never be normal again, because our minds will always return to the gas chamber, the fire pits, the death marches, the piles of dead bodies, typhoid, lice, starvation and dehumanization. I didn't have any physical problems — my scars were emotional. In our home on Friday night the Sabbath candles were lit in memory of my family.

I couldn't have asked for a better husband, a more loving and caring human being. When Rude saw how frightened I was of another war, he asked me where I wanted to go. He was very much in favor of us going to live near my sister in Israel, and we talked about this on many occasions. At that time Rude had not met any fundamentalist Jews, so it was very difficult for him to understand what people such as Fradel were like. It would not matter to her if I lived in Israel or Timbuktu, because to her I was dead. After some time he accepted my reasons for not going to Israel.

Some of the girls in the factory left Sweden and went to Canada or the United States, and I felt that part of me was leaving with them. When one of my friends, her sister, and our Hungarian friends, Güri and Iren, also decided to go to Canada, Rude suggested that we go to Canada for six months as tourists.

Perhaps I felt that if I left Europe and went far away, I would forget about the atrocities, but how can you forget Auschwitz and Bergen-Belsen? I was also hesitant to leave Europe because I might still find a family member alive somewhere, or a family member might find me. Rude had searched through the Red Cross files with no success and that failure made leaving somewhat easier. Leaving Sweden was a very emotional decision for me. I was leaving Europe behind - my country, my birthplace, where my family once lived, where Jewish people had lived for 1900 years. After we arrived in Canada, I began to realize I could not escape the memories of the pain and suffering my family must have endured. Years later as the shock wore off and reality set in, I realized that although the bodies and the ashes of my family were left behind in Europe, their spirits would always be with me.

Tragically, my brother Lazar did not survive the Holocaust. I often think of what we went through together, the pain and suffering we shared before the war. I think of what might have been had he survived. I would have had a friend and probably a larger family. We would have been able to share our lives, both the positive and negative aspects, and help each other grow spiritually. Remembrance Day is different for me than for many people. I don't know where the wind has blown my brother's ashes so I can't go anywhere to place a wreath. Although I am alone, he is with me in spirit and I will always love him.

13.

CANADA

We arrived in Halifax on April 13, 1951. We had to overlook certain things in our new country and not let them get to us. My husband had purchased first class train tickets in Sweden for the trip from Halifax to Montreal. He had paid 720 crowns more to get a night berth on the train so we'd have a nice place in which to travel. Not speaking the language, we were taken advantage of. Somebody looked at the numbers on our tickets and told us to go to a coach that had wooden benches and was certainly not first class. My husband was so angry he was just beside himself. This wasn't a very good start.

When we arrived in Montreal Güri and Iren were waiting for us. They were also Holocaust survivors, and they took us to their home, a large old house, and rented us a room there. When my husband looked at the room he didn't know whether he should put his suitcase down or just head out right away. It didn't matter very much to me, because I had slept in a lot worse places. For him, it was awful, just awful. So I said, "Okay, what can we do about this?

We'll find another place to live." The next day we
went out for a walk on St. Laurent Boulevard and as
we walked we came to a butcher shop with a cat in
the window. Well, Rude was so upset about that cat
in the window he didn't eat for a week. In Sweden
such an unhygienic thing would not be tolerated. As
a Swede, he was used to everything being neat and
clean, not haphazard as it was in Montreal. We moved
to another place in a better area, not too far from
Mount Royal and that was nice. We could walk to
the mountain in the summer.

Later we remembered that we had come here
as tourists for six months and the time was flying by.
We were supposed to go back to Sweden on October
19, 1951. We thought we should see Canada before
we went back and to do that we would have to earn
some money. We applied for work permits, which
were not difficult to get at that time. Rude got a job
at Canadair, although not in his own profession
(designing and engineering). I didn't even know what
he was doing, but he continued working in the plant
until the Korean War was over.

We didn't speak any English so we went to
the movies twice a week and listened to the words.
We even had a tutor for Rude, but he couldn't pick
up the different sounds and found the grammar
difficult. I found it interesting that although Rude was
well educated and I had no education to speak of, I
managed to learn the language more easily than he
did. Perhaps my lack of education was an asset when
it came to learning a new language.

My first job in Canada was providing homecare assistance, answering the phone and making lunch for an elderly Jewish woman who had polio and was in a wheelchair. I worked three or four hours a day for $15 a week. She was a very well educated Russian lady who had left Russia in 1919, escaping the revolution by going to Sweden. She had come to Canada in 1923, but she could still remember some Swedish and we got along very well. However, I needed a full-time job and she was very sad when I left.

I got pregnant but I didn't have a very easy time, even though I stayed home in bed. I hemorrhaged and lost the baby early in the pregnancy. It's very hard for women who have had typhoid to get pregnant and stay pregnant because typhoid scars block the tubes and make full-term pregnancy unlikely.

In our apartment building I met Kürt and Rosa, a young Hungarian couple who were Holocaust survivors and had also come to Canada from Sweden. Rosa suggested that I go to see a certain furrier on St Laurent Boulevard about a job, so I went the next day and met the manager. Although I had never worked with fur, he hired me on the spot since I knew how to sew and it was the peak of the season. I sewed in the lining by hand and was paid $160 for the first 10 days' work. To us that was a lot of money.

After the season was over I was not needed there, so I got a job as a finisher at a clothing manufacturer, Mill Craft, on St. Denise Avenue. The employees were mostly refugees like myself. When

Stalin died there was a huge celebration by the Russian and Polish Jews in the factory. We did piecework there and I was able to make good money because I could work quickly. About two years later I was promoted to inspector in my area. I stayed there until I was about six months pregnant. I came to know one of the employees, Mrs. Scharff, very well. She had a married daughter who hadn't wanted to come to Canada and had remained in Prague. Mrs. Scharff became a mother figure to me. After I went to the hospital to give birth she came to visit me and brought gifts for the baby. After I went home she came periodically and brought the baby more gifts of clothes. We had no money to buy baby clothes or for any other needs. She wasn't very happy when I told her that we might return to Sweden. She asked me why I had to go back there. She felt that Canada was a good place, but at that time it was not very good for us.

When I was only a few weeks pregnant I went to a Czechoslovakian doctor who sent me to the hospital because he wasn't sure whether I would be able to carry through this pregnancy. I went to the Royal Victoria Hospital and that was an experience in itself. As I was waiting for the doctor who had been recommended to me, a young intern and nurse came in. I was wearing winter stockings that I had brought with me from Sweden, which came up above the knee and were very warm. You did not see beautiful stockings like that in Canada. In fact, when I had arrived in Canada I noticed that the styles were way behind European styles. This young doctor and the nurse were laughing at my stockings and making fun of the way I was dressed. I couldn't say anything to them because I didn't speak enough English.

I wasn't very happy about that nurse and intern but I was happy with the doctor I got. Dr. Borne was very nice and took good care of me. Unfortunately, halfway through my pregnancy, Dr. Borne decided to go to Sweden to study uterine cancer and he sent me to another doctor, who wasn't as pleasant or as caring as Doctor Borne had been.

Then they found out that I was carrying twins. I was happy about it and just waiting for the pregnancy to end, like many other women when they get so big they don't know what to do with themselves. When I was in the hospital to give birth I became quite ill with toxemia. My husband stayed with me the whole time I was there because they didn't think I was going to make it. When the doctor in the delivery room said, "You got a boy, Mrs. Olsson!" I said, "But I have two babies." He told me that the girl had died six hours before delivery. She weighed four pounds and the boy weighed close to eight pounds. The doctor told me that had she lived she would have been very small and weak. When my husband visited me the next day he was surprised to find that they hadn't performed a Caesarian section, because the doctor had told him that they were going to do one. Perhaps if they had done that instead of waiting for the toxemia to pass, I would have had my second child. Children are a very important part of

my life. I wanted to have lots of children, but this
was not possible for me. However, I was grateful to
be alive and have the one baby.

I stayed in the hospital for ten days on a very
strict diet of salt-free food. I had a very close friend,
Inez, who came to visit me every day, and this allowed
Rude to go home and get some sleep. My treatment
in the hospital was neglectful. Was it possible this
happened because I spoke little English or French
and was a foreigner? I had decided to nurse the baby
in the hospital, but when I began to have trouble
feeding the baby, I was told to keep trying. My breast
got infected and the baby couldn't take the milk
because it had solidified. My doctor said that if the
infection didn't go away they'd give me something
to get rid of it. It didn't go away and when I went
back to the doctor he denied saying it would go away.
He said, "This isn't the bust you showed me before!"
Needless to say, I was very upset. His lack of
compassion showed his lack of commitment to the
medical profession and the oath he took as a doctor.
If he had been more caring I would have suffered a
lot less.

I had to go into the hospital to have my breast
cut and when I was waiting for the surgery to take
place, Doctor Borne came in and asked me what I
was doing there. I showed him where I had a problem
and he said, "You go home. I'll call your husband to
come and pick you up because it is not ready to be
cut. You can do the same thing at home by putting
on hot compresses." I did this, but after ten days I

was still getting worse, so this kind doctor came to the house, picked me up on a Sunday afternoon, and took me to the Royal Victoria Hospital. He performed the surgery the next morning. After the surgery he came to my bedside to reassure me. He told me that he had made a very small incision so that, "when you wear a low-cut gown the scar will not show." He re-affirmed my faith in human beings with his great compassion and sensitivity. Everyday he would come in and say, "I talked to your husband, the baby is fine." My cultural and religious background and language did not matter to him. He saw me as a human being who needed a lot of TLC. After so many negative experiences it was a great feeling to be treated with dignity, and I will always give thanks for his caring approach.

When the Korean War ended Rude was laid off from Canadair, along with 10,000 other workers and subcontractors, and he had to look for another job. It wasn't a very good time financially and I was not well. The baby got a terrible diaper rash and Rude didn't know what to do. We were renting a duplex from a very nice Hungarian couple, Josef and Anna, and Anna, who had one son herself, would come up and help my husband. We lived very contentedly even though we had no job and no money, largely because of the kind of man I was married to. We used to play a lot of cards on Friday or Saturday night with Nathan and Hella, a couple who lived nearby. They were both survivors, but they weren't Orthodox Jews, so it didn't matter if it was the Sabbath or not. We became good friends with them, and we also associated with other Swedish people.

With the Korean War over there was no job for Rude anywhere. I traveled with him to Quebec City, Hull, and Ottawa, but he could not get a job. He did qualify for $17 Unemployment Insurance Compensation (UIC) a week for eight weeks or so. We had to sell our little car, a Morris Minor, because we could not afford to pay the insurance premiums or buy gas. The most important thing for us was to pay the rent. It was an extremely difficult time. Not being well at the time, I was devastated with fear. How were we going to feed the baby? I tried to persuade my husband (which wasn't an easy job) to write to his uncle asking him to send us tickets so that we could go back to Sweden. Rude finally wrote, and his uncle arranged tickets for the three of us to return to Sweden on April 19, 1955.

How different his response was from that of my Uncle Jankev, a rabbi in New York who had ignored my plea for help in 1946. Having lost all but one of my family in the concentration camps, I wanted to go to the United States, where I had relatives — an aunt, uncle, and cousins. I had written him from Sweden asking for help getting to America, and he wrote back that I would have to wait my turn in the quota system. He didn't send any money or express sympathy or compassion for what I had gone through, or show any interest in me, his sister's daughter. In 1947 he sent me another letter telling me to leave Gustusberg immediately because my mother's soul couldn't rest in peace as long as I lived a liberal lifestyle. I was very angry and upset that he dared to mention my mother's name when he didn't care enough to help me in any way. However, his letter convinced me that my decision not to live according to Hasidic rules was the right one. I could not live in a manner that had no tolerance of diversity or respect for the right of others to live their lives as they saw fit.

I was eager to go back to Sweden, moreso than my husband. While we were waiting, the Unemployment Insurance ran out. Through friends, my husband heard that a European baker needed help two days before Christmas and two days before New Years, so he went to see him. He had to deliver bread and baskets of food on foot, special orders that people wanted at that time of year. For this he was paid 39 cents an hour. One Friday morning the baker phoned and asked why Rude hadn't come to work that morning. I told him that Rude had left three hours earlier. There was a big snowstorm in Montreal and since Rude was using public transportation it took him four hours to get to work. He was supposed to work at the bakery for two days at New Years, but when the baker called, I answered the phone and told him that I was not letting my husband go to work for him for 39 cents. He agreed to pay him 50 cents an hour. That's nothing today, but at that time every bit helped.

So there we were, living day to day, trying to make ends meet. One evening Rude's friend, Johan, who used to work with him in Sweden, called and told Rude about a company that was looking for an engineer. He went and filled out the application and three days later they called him to meet with one of the head engineers. When Rude came home he had this beautiful smile on his face and I said, "Oh, oh, I think I know why you're smiling." Sure enough, he got the job and they wanted him to start the following week. This was the middle of January 1955.

It never ceases to amaze me the role fate can play in your life. Here we had tickets to go back to Sweden in April, which would have pleased me tremendously, and my husband had finally got a job in his own profession after searching for three years. We had a big decision to make, but I couldn't make it. Rude would have to decide for all three of us. I wanted to go back and he wanted to stay. I felt that we would have more contact with his family in Sweden, but Rude said that the only thing that mattered to him was his life with me, wherever we were. We decided to stay and make our life in Montreal. Rude loved his job and it was really good for him. We bought another car, an old white Ford with the tire on the back outside of the trunk.

At the end of 1955, Rude's firm decided to move to Toronto. Rude went to Toronto for four days to look for a place for us to live. Having a baby made it very difficult for us to rent a place, but some Yugoslavian people liked Rude and let him have an apartment upstairs in their big, old house. Actually, we had two rooms, one in which the baby slept and we cooked, and the other room where we slept. We didn't mind because it was better than what we had in Montreal.

Between Christmas and New Years we moved the whole family to Richmond Hill by car. It was snowing heavily, so we found a motel for the night. There was no crib for the baby, just two single beds, so Jan slept with me. I woke up during the night and was petrified because the baby was no longer beside me. Jan had fallen off the bed and was lying between the bed and the wall. He was so tired from all the travelling that he never cried. I picked him up and we both fell deeply asleep. Exhaustion overcame our stress and our fears.

Our marriage could not have survived had we not had that strong commitment to each other as a unit — caring, sharing, always loving. I can't stress how important that is. One of my friends said that she and her husband would have pulled each other's hair out if they had gone through what we had. Rude and I not only survived; we forced ourselves to move ahead. Survival depends on having faith that survival is possible, and then supporting each other. I had learned to survive right from my mother's womb through early childhood and the death camps, so I could support my husband and give him strength. On the other hand, Rude had grown up since childhood free from the fear of war, and this allowed him to develop a peace and serenity that he shared with me. One of the most beautiful aspects of this relationship was that we could share our very different cultural backgrounds to our mutual benefit. This was only possible because we were open to each other's differences.

In 1956 we bought our first house. Jan was 19 months old. It was all very exciting! My husband did not want me go to work, as I needed to stay home with our son. Most families have grandparents or some other relative with whom they can leave the child, but not us. So it was up to us to bring the child up and I was happy to do so. I was ecstatic to go out for a walk and push that little stroller down the street or take him out to the plaza and buy an ice cream. It was a satisfying challenge and a great joy that I would never have wanted to miss. Had I gone out to work, I would have missed his first step, first word, first tooth and all that. Having a baby of my own to care for and love was a satisfying job in itself.

We did not have enough money to live on so I convinced my husband that we should rent out a room. It was not very North American to rent out a room and share a house with someone else, and certainly it wasn't very Swedish either, because they rarely needed to do that. However, we had to bend a little to get enough money to pay the mortgage. Rude finally agreed and we found a very nice Swiss man. It helped a great deal financially to rent out one room. Later on, we figured if we could manage one room, maybe we could rent out another room. The rental money from two bedrooms gave us a little extra money so that we could breathe and live comfortably.

14.

RUDE'S ACCIDENT

On February 26, 1962, while driving to work, my husband was hit head-on by a man driving a truck under the influence of alcohol. A policeman, who was our neighbor, came to my door. He asked me if I had a heart condition and when I said that I didn't, he told me that Rude had been in an accident. I stood there in shock. I couldn't think. I was numb. I didn't drive at that time, so I called my friend Jackie and we went to the Branson Hospital in North York together. It was a shocking and horrifying experience to see my husband in that smashed-up condition, with multiple injuries to the head, chest, and knee.

He had eleven doctors looking after him as a result of the multiple severe injuries. He was in that hospital from February until the third week in May. It took me an hour and a half to get to the hospital on the bus, but I made the trip every day to spend an hour and a half with him. Rude had private-duty nurses around the clock for the longest time. My mother-in-law came over from Sweden when he was released from the hospital and she stayed with us for the summer.   This was the first time that our son, Jan had any contact with a relative.

By late summer of 1962 Rude had made reasonable progress and decided to go back to the office part-time. He was a mechanical engineer, inventor and designer. He had a brilliant mind and had his life not ended at the age of 38, he would have had a wonderful future. He was designing a part that would be used in the space program. Dr. Anderson, who worked with Rude before the accident, found it difficult to accept that the damage to Rude was so severe. His parting words to me were: "What a tragedy, such a brilliant man."

As fall was approaching and the days were getting shorter, Rude had an hour's drive each way to work and it became increasingly difficult for him to see as his vision deteriorated. Around December it was no longer possible for him to drive, so I got my licence and could take him to the numerous doctors' appointments. In the fall of 1963 I was helping him into the car one day and he started to shake. That was the beginning of a convulsion. I called across the street to a neighbour, Bill Burns, who was in the x-ray department at York Central Hospital in Richmond Hill. He came running and realized Rude was having a seizure. He gave him first aid and called an ambulance. Bill helped me put Rude on the floor in the house until Dr. Zuck came. I was petrified, never having seen a grand mal seizure. Rude had one more seizure in the ambulance and another as they put him into bed. It was a terrifying experience. I rode with Rude in the ambulance and the sirens were blaring. Every time I hear sirens I think of that day. Rude stayed at Branson Hospital for about three months that time.

In the spring of 1964 I followed the doctor's suggestion and took Rude down to the Rehabilitation Centre near Sunnybrook Hospital in Toronto every day. While Rude was still at Branson the doctor advised me not to take him home, as he didn't feel I would have the strength to take care of him. He asked me if I would have any help at home and I replied, "Yes — God." The doctor wanted me to put him in a long-term care facility, but I just couldn't do it. After all we'd been through I wanted to take care of him — until death do us part. I have to live with the person who looks back at me when I look in the mirror. I can live in peace today knowing I did everything possible. Dr. McGregor, our family physician, told me in June of 1964 that he'd never met a wife who had done so much for her husband. I felt I had only done for him what he deserved, in a loving, caring way.

Several times during Rude's illness my mother came to me in my dreams and said, "Come, Esther, and I will give you bread." I haven't been able to figure out why she didn't say, "Don't cry, Ester." It was as if she offered me bread to make peace with me, to say she was sorry about not supporting me during my early childhood and teenage years.

Around 11 a.m. on June 2, the Rehab Centre called and asked me to come and take Rude home, as he wasn't doing as well as they would have liked. Actually Rude had had a small stroke while he was there. It didn't paralyze him but he was too sick to take part in the program. I picked him up at the centre and called the doctor, who ordered me to keep him in bed.

A few days later I looked out my kitchen window and saw a man in pajamas walking with a cane. My God, it was my husband Rude! He didn't know where he was. I ran out, helped him back into the house and called Dr. McGregor, who came over and made arrangements with the hospital in Richmond Hill to admit him. When I was visiting him one day he spoke to me in Swedish, "What are you doing here? Go home and look after the twins." He had lost all sense of the present.

A couple of months after that, the doctors talked to me about his condition and advised me to put him in Queen Elizabeth Hospital in Toronto. They couldn't keep him any longer in a general hospital. I was so upset that I asked my friend Maria to drive us to the hospital. It was a most horrible journey. I felt that my world was shattered and falling apart. I knew I was never going to bring him home again. The hospital was far away from our home but I went to see him every day. He wasn't there more than two or three weeks when they called and told me they'd had to take Rude by ambulance to St. Joseph's Hospital in Toronto, as they didn't have the facilities to care for him at Queen Elizabeth Hospital. They put him in a ward at first and about a week later they transferred him to a private room. He was deteriorating very rapidly. He had developed rales (the death rattle), so I knew the end was drawing near.

One day Jan asked to go to the hospital with me. When we got there Rude was unconscious, so Jan shook his dad's legs and touched his hands several times and said, "Dad wake up — it's me, Jan." The pain on our son's face was unbearable and I turned away and walked to the window. This happened on Wednesday afternoon and on Thursday, September 24, at 7:00 in the evening, my darling husband Rude Olsson was dead. I thank God that I was able to take Jan that day as that was the last time he saw his father. He was only ten and would have a long lonely road ahead of him. We had no relatives in Canada. There was no one other than me for him to turn to for help. That fall Jan had a very traumatic day at Cub Camp when Father's Day was held. On the drive home, as he told me about his feelings of loneliness and emptiness as he remembered his father, he began to cry. I put my arms around him and we cried together.

After Rude died I continued to rent out the room for some income and I stayed home and looked after Jan. I was happy that I gave him that time. I needed to give it to him because I felt that I would miss a lot if I went to work and wasn't there to watch him grow and develop every day. One Sunday night when he was 11, he came down to the family room while I was watching Ed Sullivan. I asked him why he wasn't sleeping and he said, "Mom, I can't sleep.

I'm worried. I'm thinking about what will happen to me if something happens to you." I needed to be there to reassure him and I'm glad I was. It was a very traumatic experience for him to lose his father at such a young age, especially since they were very close. My husband loved him. I have never seen anything like it. I did not get pregnant until the fifth year of our marriage, and when my son was born my husband said, "Oh, how I wish we would have had him earlier." That's the joy we both got from this baby. The sun shone on all of us just having him.

During the long period when Rude was so ill and in the hospital, my friend Joan, asked me how I could still smile so much. I said, "Joan, I have two choices. I can lie down and die with this man or I can go on living. My choice is to go on living. I have a son to raise and if I cannot smile it is not good for my son or me . Really, there isn't much choice, is there?" I raised my boy in the best way I knew.

15.

FRADEL

In late 1947, while I was at work in Gustavsberg, Sweden, I received a phone call from David, a Russian Jew, who told me that he was going to marry my sister. I was shocked because I'd never had contact with him before and they had not invited me to their wedding. I didn't understand why he was even calling me if I was not to be invited to the wedding, but I realized later that he had called me to satisfy the Hasidic tradition of getting permission for marriage from an older sibling when the parents were dead. Since Fradel was three years younger than me she was required to get this permission from me. The brief phone call resolved nothing, but the attempt had been made and religious tradition had been satisfied. I didn't care who she married. Remembering all that my sister and I had gone through during the war, not being invited to the wedding left me numb, furious and sad. Eighty-seven members of our family had perished during the war — parents, brothers, sisters, cousins, uncles and aunts. I was the only member of our family still alive to share her joy, but she rejected me because I wouldn't follow her religious beliefs. Fradel didn't ostracize me just because I worked on the Sabbath. She saw that I had a Swedish boyfriend and realized I wasn't going to live my life according to the Hasidic rules that our parents had made us follow at home. I was hurt for the longest time and wondered how she could be so selfish and cruel.

I heard from others that my sister and her husband moved to Denmark and then went to Israel after their marriage. I did not hear from them at all. I only saw my sister once after we were liberated from Bergen-Belsen and got to Sweden. We were together that summer in that beautiful summer resort outside Gustavsberg, but she spent her time with Orthodox religious girls, while I preferred the company of more liberated people. Then my sister went to Fairnabrook to learn Hebrew. At home the girls spoke only Yiddish, because in the Hasidic tradition only the males learn Hebrew, which is the language used for prayer. I wasn't interested in going to Fairnabrook, as I wanted independence, not more control.

I saw her in the spring of 1946 at Passover. She brought her own matzah and hard-boiled eggs, probably thinking that since I wasn't kosher, my kitchen wouldn't be kosher either. She wouldn't eat anything from my place, just water, and she didn't stay overnight. I did not and do not celebrate Passover; I prefer to celebrate life. I cannot celebrate something that happened over 2000 years ago. However, I can celebrate an event that happened in the last century: the end of the Nazis' horrendous crime against humanity. I don't have personal knowledge of the Egyptian exodus, but I know exactly what happened on April 15 1945 because I was there.

Another celebration I have trouble with is Purim. This celebrates the death of Haman, who had been appointed Prime Minister to the King of Persia. It is said that one Jewish leader refused to bow to Haman, who then plotted to annihilate all the Jews in Persia. Through the efforts of Ester the plot failed and Haman and his family were hanged. I feel very strongly that Purim should be updated 2300 years in order to celebrate the destruction in 1945 of Adolph Hitler, the modern-day Haman whose plot did succeed in killing six million Jews and five million others, including invalids, homosexuals and Gypsies. I believe that children today must be taught about Hitler if we are to prevent this from happening again.

When Fradel visited me for one day in the spring of 1946, she gave me a book that someone in Denmark had given to her. I recognized it immediately as my father's first book. I was shocked because to my knowledge most Jewish literature had been burned or destroyed. I made a decision not to give it back to my sister at that time. I felt that since I was the oldest family survivor I had more right to it. I would accept the responsibility of preserving it and having it translated from Yiddish to English. So far I have not been successful in finding a translator, but I know I will. My feelings toward my father are very negative because he prevented me from growing as I needed to and being part of the larger universe outside the small cocoon in which we lived. Now I want to have his book translated so that I can share his thoughts. Much later my cousin in New York sent me another of my father's books. It is written in Old Hebrew with no translation that I know of. This book has parts of four different books that he had written in the 1930s. It means a lot to me since this book is a direct connection to my family that once existed. I must preserve it for my grandchildren, as it's a connection to their past as well. I am putting my negative feelings aside by preserving part of my father's journey. Perhaps this will turn a negative into a positive. I doubt that these books would ever be translated into any other language if they hadn't fallen into my possession. It would be a great loss but this is largely the fault of the Hasidic religion for isolating their language from any other language.

I did not see Fradel again until 1982 in Boston. In the spring of 1982 my son asked me to get in touch with my sister. I tried to explain what the Hasidim are like and that she would not want anything to do with me, but he felt that she might have changed since the war. I wondered if he wanted me to contact her for his benefit or mine. He might have wanted to expand his family by renewing family connections. I agreed to write. Some years earlier I had received a letter from my brother-in-law, David. He had been at a medical conference in France and travelled to Sweden to try and find me. My friend Edith told him that Rude and I had left for Canada and she gave him our address in Montreal. He wrote me and their return address in Israel was on the envelope. For all those years I had kept the letter but not answered it. When Fradel received my letter she wrote to tell me that she and her husband would be in Boston in April, as their youngest son, Haim, would be studying divinity at Harvard University. I had been given my nephew's phone number in Boston, so I called to make arrangements to meet them in the first week of May 1982.

Meanwhile, Jan was going to be in Boston in April as part of a Queen's University educational tour, so he arranged to meet them in the third week of April. When Jan came home from Boston he told me that they had tried to bribe him to leave home, promising to finance his studies completely. I assume this would include moving to Israel and leading their way of life, although they didn't discuss this. I felt betrayed that my sister would attempt to take my own flesh and blood away from me. This might be what her religious beliefs told her was right, but surely this is not what God would want.

On May 2, 1982 I arrived in Boston. I finally saw my sister again after 36 years, along with her husband, son and daughter-in-law. Fradel had ten children, but the son who was present was the only one who knew he had an aunt who had survived the Holocaust with their mother. All her children are Hasidic except this youngest son, Haim. Strangely, her husband David is not Hasidic either. The other sons spent most of their days in the synagogue while their wives were out working. She showed me pictures of the other nine children, but all she talked about was their religious lives. Fradel expressed her pride in them and wished our parents could share her joy.

During dinner I told my sister that in Toronto I had talked to a rabbi from Szatmar, our hometown in Hungary. This rabbi was very liberal and had a large multi-racial and multi-religious congregation. He was open to and tolerant of other religions and said he would perform the Jewish marriage rituals for me if I wanted to get married. He felt that marriage should include rather than exclude people. I was excited to share this information with Fradel, hoping it might bring us closer together, but she started laughing and said to her husband, "Husband, did you hear this? Is this a rabbi? He is no rabbi." There was silence at the table. Clearly only Orthodox beliefs and believers were of any value to her.

We were supposed to walk around the university after dinner, but it started to rain, so my nephew and I went to a coffeehouse and had a three-hour dialogue. His main concern was that I not hurt his mother. How would I do this? She had already hurt herself by ignoring God's Golden Rule: Love one another as we love ourselves. I couldn't condone her behaviour or forgive her for denying my existence to her family. I wondered if she had performed shiva, the ritual of sitting on the floor for seven days mourning the dead. She would have had to sit alone since nine of her children didn't know I existed. I have asked God to forgive her; it's between God and her. I knew that in order to free myself of anger I had to forgive her.

My nephew asked me what I would tell God when he called me home and I told him I would tell my God that I did the job he sent me down to do. He also wanted to know if his grandfather was a saint. I told him that my father was a human being with strengths and weaknesses. These two subjects were his only concern; there was no talk about his family, his studies or his life. As we parted at closing time he told me that he could understand my choice of a liberal lifestyle if it was the result of the horrors of the Holocaust. I told him I had been looking for a more open and tolerant way of life long before the war started.

When we met again the next morning my sister announced in front of everyone that she could not accept me as part of her family, "I cannot be any different than our father would have been." I was devastated to hear her cruel words and be humiliated in front of my family. It was so unnecessary for me to travel from Toronto to Boston to suffer such cruel treatment. She knew what my lifestyle was before I went there, so I have to wonder what her real motives were in asking me to come to Boston. I didn't understand why she would want to cause me more pain by denying my existence, just because I didn't follow her religious beliefs. Why do people continue to cause so much pain for each other because of cultural, racial, religious, or national differences? I was very sad but I realized that Fradel had to live her life according to her beliefs and could not accept me because I was so alien to her. Fradel lives the way my parents lived, not giving an inch or bending, and this reflects her interpretation of the messages she received at home. I also knew that I had to live my life as I saw fit. The life I am living reflects my lifelong desire for a more flexible way of life. I got up from the table and left for good.

I have often wondered about my sister's behaviour. When I look back on our lives as children I can see the childhood tapes she made then. Each night Fradel would kick up a fuss about going to bed and my father would pick her up and place her in his bed. He would lie down beside her until she had fallen asleep and then place her in Mama's bed for the night. I can see how the strong bond that resulted from this nighttime habit affected her later in life. Her intolerance of those who are different originated with our father. Perhaps she wanted to replace my father and control my life as he tried to do.

I had to accept the fact that in spite of all we endured and survived together, her attitude toward me had not changed. I feel very sorry for her children and grandchildren living in that negative, controlling environment. Perhaps some of her grandchildren will break away and see the bigotry her fundamentalist beliefs encourage. They may discover the difference between religious beliefs and true spirituality and faith. When my grandchildren started to ask questions, I believed they deserved to be told the whole truth. I told them that my sister had survived the Holocaust with me but now denied my existence because I had married a non-Jew, their grandfather. I have been able to tell my grandchildren the truth about our family and help them see the difference between faith and religion. They have already begun to ask me about religious beliefs and I am happy to be able to answer their questions without religious bias. My grandchildren will know what is important to me and what should be important in their lives. In the end they are the only ones who can decide what is important to them.

It is my hope that as they mature they will always have open minds and be sensitive to other people's feelings, beliefs and religious or cultural differences. I hope they will be able to see beyond physical, racial, religious and cultural differences and have faith in all good people. But first they must have faith in themselves. I hope I can encourage them to be loving and caring toward all mankind. My sister's family life is controlled by their religion and they have lost faith in their ability to make their own decisions about their lives.

In August that year my nephew Haim phoned and said, "You mean more to me than just an aunt." He told he would come to Jan's wedding me if my son married a Jewish girl. He also told me that his family was returning to Israel and he would soon follow them. I have not heard from him since then; he was probably influenced to cease all contact with me. He sounded genuine, but on reflection I could see that his comments were conditional and manipulative, very similar to his mother's point of view.

16.

BEING DIFFERENT

I'm still puzzled about what made me different from the rest of my siblings. Of the six children only my younger brother Lazar and I had liberal ideas and wanted to choose our own way of living. What made us different from the others? Today we understand more about how genetic factors affect our lives, and are trying to find out what part comes from nature and what part comes from nurture. We were taught to be honest, caring, and truthful. My father said that if he caught us lying he would cut our tongues out. We were told that lying was against God's law and yet we saw our parents lie numerous times when it suited their needs. Each year they would lie to the inspector as they told him there were no school-aged children in our home. When I questioned my parents — "Why can't I…? Why must I…? Why do I have to…?" — the answer was always the same: "The Talmud is not to be questioned." Four of my siblings never questioned my parents; they accepted their teaching with blind faith, something Lazar and I couldn't do. Perhaps my brother and I were less intimidated by our father's use of threats, physical punishment, and fear of God's punishment for lying, disrespect, or disobedience. I see now how negative this type of teaching can be in a family. Being taught not to lie through fear is a negative. Being taught to tell the truth because it is the right thing to do is a positive.

Fortunately I was able to turn those negative teachings into positive guidelines. In my home I learned that I should not lie or steal. Mama used to say that if somebody throws a stone at you, throw bread back. Early in my life I learned the importance of sharing, caring and honesty. That backbone, that strength, gave me the spirit to branch out, make my own decisions about what was right and wrong, and develop as the person I needed to be. Even as a young teenager I wanted to mix with other people and ask them what they were thinking, what their lives were like.

A Jewish girl who lived not too far from us used to walk by our house on her way to the *gymnasium*, the high school. She was older than I was and carried a beautiful briefcase. I was so envious, wondering what she was learning. Why couldn't I go there too? I'm still angry that I was deprived of an education. When my son was 12 years old, he said it was too bad that I was not educated, because I could have been a good lawyer. He thought my education had been interrupted because of the war, but I was still in denial, unable to tell him the real reason I had no education.

Fradel and I came from the same family, ate the same food, had the same mother and father. Why are we so different? When I returned home from Boston I was still devastated by her treatment of me. Later I realized how fortunate I was because I fought to be able to be free to choose how to live my life. I wondered what Fradel could share with me other than her religious beliefs. On the other hand I could share ideas, thoughts, spirituality, and beliefs with her. I don't live just for me because that's not enough. I need to share with other people whatever I can — time, a pot of good soup, a loaf of bread, whatever I have. Even just a friendly greeting: "Good morning, how are you? It's a beautiful day. Are you feeling okay?" That's sharing that comes from the heart.

I believe in the influence of genetic factors and I want to know more about myself, where my personality characteristics came from. I'm sure a lot of it comes from my parents. Even today I do some things the same way as Mama did. I have my father's skin colouring and curly hair. Grandfather Jankev, my father's father, had a philosophical side, as I do. My father's first cousins were modern, well-mannered ladies. I never saw them with a prayer book in their hand. Most of the members of my father's family were modern Jews so he infrequently spoke of them. He wanted no modern influence on his children. My parents were worried that we might adopt these outside influences as our own.

My mother-in-law in Sweden once asked me why I was so different from the other refugee girls. I haven't yet figured out why I am different. Perhaps it's just different genes — my attitude and spirituality probably come from my paternal grandfather and great-grandfather. My Uncle Joseph was not very religious and his children were more modern than he was. My Aunt Margaret was very different from my mother. Is this why my parents had difficulty with me? As much as I loved and respected them, and never talked against them, I believed firmly in live and let live. I could not understand how they could be so angry that Lazar and I were more liberal in our thinking. So much slaughter and destruction was going on all around us, and evil people had already annihilated millions. My brother and I were good kids, yet we were being severely disciplined for going to a movie.

17.

DENIAL

I lived in denial for almost fifty years because I thought I could hide. I didn't want anybody to know who I was. I figured that if they didn't know my story, they couldn't hurt my son or me. My neighbours knew me as a nice Hungarian woman who minded her own business and enjoyed gardening. I kept my mouth closed because I had this fear that if they knew who I was they wouldn't like my son or me. If they knew who I was they might hurt us. I felt I had already paid the price for my son as well as for myself.

In Richmond Hill I came to know Pastor Meyers because his wife and I sewed neckerchiefs for the cub troop at the church. One day when the pastor called on me at home I told him about my past, including the time in the camps. He told me that his grandfather was a German Jew. He asked me to speak to his congregation, which had a large number of Germans in it. He approached me many times on this matter, but I always said no because I was afraid there might be Nazis hiding in the congregation. The fear of having people know I was a Jew and the possible effect on my son kept me from speaking to his congregation. Today I wish I had acted differently and accepted his offer. Of course, today I am much stronger.

I fear the reappearance of a Nazi regime, and I still fear those people who collaborated with Hitler. They took away our food, our homes, our families and our self-dignity. Those of us who had spiritual strength and faith suffered like the rest, but we seemed to have a better ability to cope with and survive in such a jungle. Others had no chance to use their spiritual strength to survive — they were taken straight from the train to the gas chamber. They didn't even have time to give up. There are various levels of spiritual strength. Some prisoners survived for quite a while and then committed suicide. Others died of starvation or disease, which no amount of spirituality or faith can prevent.

After my husband's death I withdrew into myself. Later I realized that when I locked myself in, I locked others out of my life. The births of my grandchildren enabled me to unlock the doors from within and now I am reaping the fruits of sharing my most intimate life with others.

Today I am dealing with my fears in a more positive way. Now that I am involved with grandchildren I realize how important it is for them to know the complete truth. Being blessed with wonderful grandchildren has given me more strength and courage to continue my mission to speak out against intolerance and bigotry. Brenna, my oldest granddaughter, encouraged me to speak at her elementary school. I have also been grateful for the opportunity I have been given to speak to the students at other elementary and high schools. The positive feedback from the students is overwhelming. Letters from them indicate that they want me to return and I will. I have made a commitment to myself to speak for the millions of victims who cannot speak for themselves. I know that I cannot carry the voices of one and a half million children, but if I can touch even one child and help this child become more tolerant of others, I will be grateful.

I feel there is more tolerance in Canada today then there was 40 years ago. I must speak up and help this tolerance spread so children of the world will not suffer again. I found out that I couldn't hide forever, living in denial. Sooner or later I had to come out of hiding, even though it is painful every time I speak about my past.

Perhaps I survived because of my faith and my dream of living in a cabin in the woods where nobody could find me. Part of my dream came true. Until recently I had a cottage north of Toronto and I stayed up there, high on a hill. There weren't many people around, nobody knew who I was, and I thought I could live there happy and contented. However, the nighttimes weren't so happy. I paid plenty for keeping everything inside me. I kept having the same nightmare in which I was hiding or running from the SS as they came to round us up. Every night I relived what I had endured in the camps. I saw that my silence was causing me more harm than good. I needed to come out of my shell with the help of caring friends and share my experiences with them and others, not just what I had endured during the war but also when I was a young child, struggling to grow and develop in the repressive Hasidic environment. Now I live in an environment I have chosen that suits my soul, and I am able to speak more freely of my past.

It's still a painful process. I feel hurt and bewildered when I think of being rejected by the country where I was born, rejected by the Nazi savages who came in, occupied the country, and subjected us to those horrific ordeals. Still, I count my blessings daily because I have endured a lot less than some of my people. Being rejected by my younger sister, whom I sheltered and helped to survive, has been very difficult to deal with. However, over time I have come to see that she rejected me because of the Hasidic belief that their way is the only way. I became a non-person because I refused to live according to their beliefs. Ironically, that's the way it was when the Nazis marched us to the train to Auschwitz. There we had no choice either — we had to do what they wanted or get beaten or shot.

Many Holocaust survivors still carry their pain in silence. I was silent for many years, not because of pain, but out of fear for my child, how his peers would treat him, and how he would relate to my personal suffering. At that time I thought that I was making the right decision but I realize now that I was wrong. I needed to learn to share my pain as well as my joy with my family and friends. Perhaps the families of survivors want to hear about the pain and suffering. Knowing that others care could help ease the survivor's pain. On the other hand, some survivors have put a terrible burden on their families by overpowering their children with stories of what they have endured. The result has often been children filled with feelings of great guilt and anger. One of these children said to me, "Why doesn't my mother just forget the past and move on with her life?" At first this type of question angered me, but then I realized that this child lacked understanding and compassion. How could any survivor forget such a horrendous past? For a survivor life can never be normal again, not because we're crazy but simply because every day there's something that reminds us of the Holocaust. When I was in denial I hoped that if I didn't speak of the atrocities I could avoid or deaden the pain. I realized later that I had to accept the fact that my family was brutally murdered as part of a systematic, premeditated plan that also saw the deaths of millions of other people. Survivors must share their pain, in spite of their fears of rejection or reprisal, even though it causes them more suffering to do so. We survivors pay a high price whatever we decide to do. I chose not to be silent anymore.

My father was very protective and wouldn't let me go places because he was afraid I might be hurt. I had the same kind of feelings about my son but did not follow them to the same extent as my father. I can see today how important it is to give our

children the opportunity to expand their experiences
and to allow them the space to grow spiritually and
mature emotionally. Their spirits must be cultivated
and nourished. We must never lose faith in our
children and grandchildren, for they will take with
them on their journey what we gave to them. I gave
my son freedom, the freedom I never had. I gave my
son enough elbowroom so that he could spread out
and have a larger perspective of the world around
him.

The only thing I sheltered him from was my
past experiences in the death camps. I did not want
him to be sad about what I'd gone through. A man I
met recently was surprised that I had a different view
of life and philosophy than his parents, who were
survivors. He said he wished his parents were more
like me. He felt they'd ruined his life and his sister's.
"Every day we heard what they went through, what
they had endured, what they had to do and what they
couldn't do. Day in and day out they burdened us."
He found it extremely stressful to grow up in such a
dysfunctional family and he wished his parents would
get some counseling. I am glad I didn't do that to
my son. I wanted him to grow up as natural and free
as possible. I listened to him and was prepared to
answer any questions he had. The times weren't
always great but we made the best of it and he got
the education he required.

All we survivors have left are memories of the
dead, especially what they endured and how they
died. When I think about Mama and her three little

grandchildren, Judy, Cathy, and Hedy, going into the gas chamber, along with my sister Regina and sister-in-law with their children, my pain is indescribable. I wonder what their thoughts were near the end. It's still not easy dealing with those haunting memories.

One night not too long ago, I dreamed that my little six-and-a-half-year-old granddaughter, Alexandra Leah, and I were hiding. I said to her, "Come, come, let's run. The SS are coming." When my grandchildren ask me, "Did you have a good night, Bubba?" I cannot always tell them the truth and say, "No, sweetheart, I didn't. I had a terrible nightmare." However, sometimes I can answer their questions honestly. Recently Alexandra came home from school and told me she had a new friend called Serena, and I told her that my sister Sarah's name was Serena in Hungarian. She asked me if my sister had died in the war. I said that she had died in the hospital during the war, leaving three children under the age of four. When Alexandra asked me if these children were killed in the war, I said yes, but didn't tell her any details. Then she asked," What kind of people would hurt little children? Little children don't hurt anyone." I could only reply, "Sick people."

We have to care about and share with our neighbours next door and around the world. When we are not able to share we isolate ourselves from the rest of the world. We become greedy; we want to stay by ourselves. People who lock people out lock themselves in. I hope and pray that the young people who read these lines will understand my message.

It's not always easy being Hungarian and having to say things in English. It's important for me to tell my story and I appreciate people listening to me. I have been talking to students in grades seven and eight and high school and I can tell by the letters they write me that they were listening. I hope my message stays with them and they can apply it to their lives. I have been overwhelmed by the feedback I received in their letters.

After Rude's death in 1964 I had gone to see a Scottish psychiatrist in Toronto who was the therapist of a friend of mine. I explained why I was there, what I had been through, and I talked about Rude and myself. I spoke to him of my fears, how I didn't know what I was going to do now that Rude was gone. I had no education. I wasn't trained for any job. I didn't speak English very well and couldn't write it. I was concerned because I was left with a young boy to raise. He had no difficulty understanding why I had married a Gentile once he heard what kind of man Rude was.

While I was waiting for this appointment a young man had come out of the office with red, wet eyes. The doctor told me that the man was one of 50 patients who were Holocaust survivors and all of them were having a difficult time dealing with life. He said I puzzled him because I wasn't having a hard time with anything other than Rude's death. The doctor wondered why I had such a well-balanced attitude compared to some of the other survivors he treated. He said most people who have had a lot of tragedy in their lives feel that the world owes them a living. I did not feel that way. I owed myself a living. I had to look after my child and me.

Why was I not having the same problems as the other survivors? Could it be that my past life was secondary because the center of my life was my son and his father? When I have been talking to other survivors I have noticed that many of them have extremely negative attitudes. They have chosen to remember only the negative parts of their past and this makes it difficult for them to find a balance in their lives. I find a balance by remembering both the positive as well as the negative aspects, and I'm sure that there are other survivors who have found balance that way too. I have difficulty becoming friends or maintaining friendships with some survivors because I need to be with people who have more positive attitudes. When my time was up I asked the psychiatrist if he wanted to see me again and he said, "No, not as a patient, anyway."

Thirty-four years later I had the urge to contact him and located him and his wife through my dear friend, Jackie. The four of us got together at his home and he still remembered me after all those years. His first comment was, "My, my, haven't we grown up! Have you finally worked it out why you married a Gentile?" I replied that I didn't remember having any problem with that decision. He commented that he now had a Christian son-in-law whom he loved dearly.

After that visit I was on cloud nine. Seeing him again was the highlight of my year. He told me he was very happy that I had made the choice to speak to young students and to write my book.

18.

FREEDOM

Freedom has all kinds of connotations and means different things to different people. We're free to choose what kind of clothes we want to wear, what colour of paint we are going to buy, what schools our children go to, what kind of car we buy, what kind of hat we want. Those things represent the freedom of daily choices and it's great to have that freedom, but to know what freedom really is, you have to have it taken away from you. I had it one day and the next day it was taken away for a long, long time. Freedom should not be taken for granted. Freedom for me means being able to walk down the street without fear, live in a beautiful country that stands for freedom, do whatever I like, share my experiences with you. In some countries that wouldn't be possible, but I am grateful to live in a country where all this freedom exists. I am not talking about a selfish kind of freedom where people break rules because they feel like it, endangering others by their actions. Most restrictions are just common sense, and obeying rules doesn't mean losing our freedom. There is no such thing as one hundred percent freedom. With freedom of choice and the freedom to be ourselves, we should take each day as it comes and treat it with respect.

Years after Rude's death I finally realized that it would be impossible to replace him with any other man. One person cannot replace another because we all have our different strengths and weaknesses. I have discovered through my journey that most of the strengths and weaknesses are self-determined. God gave us free will, so most of the time we are in charge of our own futures. In the death camps the Nazis dehumanized us as much as they could and took control away from us. When the Allies liberated me on April 15, 1945, l regained control of my life and was again responsible for steering my vessel in the right direction, not letting it sink or run aground.

I firmly believe that I am both the container and the contained. The doors to heaven and hell are locked from the inside and each individual holds both keys. God's gift of free will gives each of us the ability to choose good or evil by unlocking either door from the inside. In early Hebrew, Yahweh means "God within." Before Abraham, Jews believed that God (Yahweh) was within themselves. Then religions separated God from man, putting God up in heaven and us down below on earth. This gave them someone to blame when things went wrong; famine, flood, and war became God's responsibility. I believe that the responsibility for atrocities such as the Holocaust lies with mankind, because we have free will and can choose to do good or evil. In the beginning each individual was the vessel, and faith and God were the captains of that vessel. When God was placed in Heaven only faith remained. That is why I say we must not lose faith in ourselves. We are in charge of our vessels. Our spirit must be the driving force. Spirituality inspires enthusiasm. To me a lack of enthusiasm indicates a lack of spirituality.

If we don't have respect for freedom, my concern is that greed and religious differences will rise again and history could very well repeat itself. My concern is not for me but for our grandchildren and future generations. I hope that the next generation will do better than we did and not allow such atrocities to happen again. We must respect our freedom, love it, and care for it. Then we can live our lives without being worried about somebody coming along and taking that freedom away from us. I can't imagine myself not having it again because I know what it's like having it taken away and living without it. My parents denied me freedom of choice, but I learned later in the camps what the complete loss of freedom means. I still have a hard time dealing with the fear of losing my freedom. We must free our children, our grandchildren and ourselves of that fear.

I did not feel free for many years. Even though I was free to choose how I wanted to live my life I was not free of the brutal memories of the atrocities of the war —gas chambers, fire pits, typhoid and lice — and the loss of my family. I will probably never be free of these memories.

19.

RELIGION

I was brought up in an environment of religious isolation. We were taught to believe that religion was the most important element of our existence. As I matured spiritually and intellectually I became aware that spirituality and faith were stronger and more meaningful to me than religion. I saw that faith and spirituality had to come from within, while religions were man-made institutions that were imposed from without. Perhaps this was the beginning of my view that God was separate from religion and resided inside of us, not up in heaven. As my feelings about this got stronger I had no doubt about the way I wanted to live: true to my own beliefs, not those imposed by someone else's religion.

Religion didn't save anyone from the atrocities during the war. I saw ultra-religious Jews praying to prepare themselves for death rather than working to survive. On the other hand, I was able to share my faith with some of my fellow prisoners and give them hope of survival.

There is a story told by many survivors about an incident that took place in one of the death camps.

Some of the prisoners decided to put God on trial for allowing the Holocaust to happen. During the trial one of the prisoners cried out to God, "Why did you not send us some help?" It is said that God replied, "I did. I sent you." My interpretation of this story is that God didn't create the Holocaust, people did, so it's up to us to prevent another Holocaust from occurring. I believe that God wants us survivors to spread the message of tolerance and acceptance to all people, especially the next generation.

It would be impossible for me to live on religion alone, as my parents did, because religion is narrow and restrictive, while faith is limitless and has no boundaries. Having faith in God's will and commandments has given me the strength to maintain my faith in humanity and helps free me of many of my fears of the past and the present. It is important to have faith and embrace it, for without it our lives and our souls would be empty. My faith allows me to do unto others as I would have them do unto me. This is the way my God would want me to be.

A few years ago I had a conversation with a priest in Richmond Hill who tried to convince me that his religion was the only true religion. I compared religion to antibiotics, because both are man-made. Not every antibiotic works for every person. Some people are allergic to certain antibiotics but respond favorably to others. Adults search for religions that suit their souls. We need only remember the Ten Commandments and the Golden Rule while we search. The priest became terribly upset with my feelings about religion. When I told him that he needed to be more tolerant of other religions and more open to other opinions he ended the conversation by hanging up the phone. He seemed unable to understand or accept that all religions grew from one main root. As the tree grew it developed many limbs and branches developed from those limbs. Some of these branches grew in different directions while some branches remained close to the main trunk. If all religions stem from one basic root system, then why are there so many religions and so many religious wars and so much destruction in the name of religion? Long before there were nations, when we were all just tribes, people believed in many gods.

Based on my experiences I believe that religion is focused more on culture and politics than on God, and this seems to be true of religions throughout the world. I acknowledge that cultural differences are very important in shaping our characters but to me faith is even more important. Having faith allows me to be tolerant of other religions and cultures I encounter and accept all races and colours. Being able to separate faith and religion makes it possible for me to accept and respect all religions and share my views and my faith with everyone. I don't like it when others make racist, sexist or discriminatory remarks around me. People who make such remarks or behave in a bigoted way do not have faith in themselves or in a higher power. They lack faith and spirituality, the two most important ingredients in life.

To me the Hasidim are trying to go backward

in time. Their ultra-conservatism has been rejected
by most other Jews, but they remain strong now in
the United States and Israel. Recently I viewed a
television program from New York on the Vision
Network about the Hasidic way of life. Some of the
people interviewed were from Szatmar, my
hometown. The most interesting part for me was a
young woman who had left the Hasidic life to become
a writer. I could relate to her because she wanted to
go to university, and in Hasidim women are not
allowed to do this. They're not supposed to mix
with others, especially men. It made me realize how
fortunate I was to have the strength to decide for
myself the kind of life I did not want to live.

When I was about ten, some kids on the street
threw stones at my father one Saturday morning as
he was walking to the synagogue. This annoyed him,
of course, but even then I was bothered by the fact
that my parents had to wear such different clothing
— fur hats and long black robes. God didn't say
what you should wear, or that you should walk
around making a spectacle of yourself. You can love
God and live according to his commandments while
you are dressed the same as your neighbor. Is it not
the internal that counts, what we are inside? I can put
a ton of makeup on my face and still be the ugliest
woman inside. Who am I kidding? I am only fooling
myself.

I am not condoning the children's behaviour
for one minute; no one has the right to throw stones
at another human being. This behaviour is picked up

in the home. What they hear and see is how they are going to behave outside the home. But when I saw a Hasidic man on the TV program, it could have been my father, or older brother, Martin, because that's exactly what they looked like. I could not sympathize with the men, but I felt compassion for the young woman because she was in limbo. She couldn't break away completely because from time to time she went to see her parents. They have not ostracized her because she has not married yet. Perhaps she'll choose to stay single or marry within her religion; otherwise she will not be able to see her parents.

My situation was different. After the war I married for love and companionship. My sister, Fradel, and my Uncle Jankev believe that I married "out of my faith," but nothing could be further from the truth. The man I married was born into a different religion. None of us has a choice in that matter. However, I know we both had the same faith and believed in the same God. For me faith does not have to be connected to religion. I have faith in God, but not in a religion that is created by man and often used for political or personal gain. If I want, I can change my religion many times during my life. I have friends whose partners have changed their religions for social reasons or to meet parental demands. I do not care about the religious beliefs of my friends. I am interested in them as people, not their religion.

Even as a child I believed that I would be all right, in spite of my parents' disapproval of me. As I grew older this belief developed into a faith in myself

that carried me through the war and gave me hope
that I would survive the concentration camps. As a
teenager I had decided that when I got married I would
never live at home or in the same city as my parents.
I would live far away because I was not going to
submit to their religious rituals such as cutting my
hair off, a ritual Hasidic women have to perform the
morning after their wedding. This ritual started with
Solomon's adulterous wife but I never understood
what it had to do with me, nor did I ever want to
have that experience. I did not want to live hairless
or without freedom of choice for the rest of my days.
Ironically, when we arrived in Auschwitz one of the
first things the Nazis did was shave our hair off.

20.

TEACHING CHILDREN

Some children are brought up in homes where they learn negative attitudes, especially racism and bigotry. One summer I decided to make peach jam so I went to a market in Toronto where many European people shopped. I lined up for the longest time at the checkout because it was so busy. A woman and her daughter came along and stepped in line in front of me. I said, "Excuse me, I was here long before you. I have been waiting for a long time." The woman really lit into me: "I know your kind. You people come here and take our place away from us." I guess she wanted to buy something and get out quickly, and all of us "European people" were in her way. I didn't know where to turn or where to look, as there were lots of people standing there listening. However, she had to hear what I had to say. I said, "Really, how do you know me? I'm white like you, also my blood is red like yours! But you know something? You are very ignorant. I feel sorry for your daughter who has to grow up in the negative and bigoted environment you provide for her." Now what kind of tape does a girl like that make with such a racist mother? Yes, I came from Europe, but so did her ancestors. When I was finished with her, the look on her face and the face of the little girl told me she wished that she had never opened her mouth. One should not waste too much energy on this kind of person, but one cannot afford to ignore them either. Perhaps when something negative happens to them they will remember what they have done to other people.

We must fight racism, anti-Semitism and bigotry at every opportunity. We must not walk away from the slightest racist remark or action. When we walk away quietly we appear to condone the action or comment. We must fight it wherever we find it, especially in schools, in the community and at home. Only then can we hope to achieve peace, tolerance and love for mankind. Years ago Rude and I were visiting another couple in Montreal and the two men were talking about car ownership. I heard our friend say to my husband, "I don't understand why Mr. Anderson would buy a Buick; only Jews buy Buicks." His body language showed that he was angry that his boss would buy a Buick. After we left and were in the car, my husband said to me, "Why did you not speak up?" I said, "What's the point?" Rude, on the other hand, was very upset that his friend would express such racist thoughts.

Bigotry based on colour, religion, age, height, size, sexual orientation, gender and cultural differences can take many subtle forms. In my opinion bigotry is nothing more than ignorance where people put someone else down in order to feel better about themselves. Children are not born bigots. When bigotry is all around them in homes, schools, churches and synagogues, how can a child avoid being influenced? I still recall German children standing on the sidewalks watching us march by. One little boy shouted, *"Muter, Muter* — Mother, Mother, come and see. The idiots are coming."* It's in our best interest to be aggressive about teaching our children tolerance, respect, compassion and understanding.

My sympathies go out to those who, like me, are being ostracized because they choose to live their lives free, outside religious boundaries. I tell them that if they have faith and believe in themselves they can believe in a higher power. I heard about a little orphan girl who was taken from Poland to Russia in 1945, while her brother remained in Poland. He did not want to be a Jew any longer because of all the persecutions he had endured. Later, when his sister returned to Poland, she renounced him, just as my sister renounced me. Maybe someday she will regret being so judgmental toward a member of her family. We must also be careful not to judge these people who have ostracized us or carry anger in our hearts towards them. They have to live with their decision every day.

We have to believe in and love ourselves, and get on with our lives. If we do this we can never go wrong. Believe me, I've been through it. I know who I am and that will protect me from those people who want to impose their way of living on me. Perhaps

God can forgive them. Unlike them, I do not presume to speak for God. Bigoted people think they alone know what God has said, but I know that being judgmental is not God's will. I see God as a non-judgmental entity, a benevolent mother/strong father figure. I call fundamentalists bigots because their way of life often promotes bigotry. I respect their right to choose their own way of life, but I do not accept their intolerance of other ways of living and I don't want to live their narrow-minded lifestyle.

It is not God's will that our brothers and sisters denounce us. He wants us to live together as one people, regardless of where we were born or what family we were born into. Our religion should not matter. Whatever we believe in — ourselves, the Law of the Universe, or something far greater than that — is fine, as long as we are good human beings and have caring, loving souls. My God has really looked after me and guided me in the direction that was right for me. There's something higher and stronger than I am, so I can't give up. I still have hope today, as I did when I was in the underground bunker in Essen. I hoped then that I would survive, get out of it and be well. I still have that strong faith.

Recently I accompanied grade 10 and 12 students on a field trip to the Holocaust Centre in Toronto. We also went to a synagogue where we were given a lecture on different Jewish religious groups — reform, conservative, liberal, Orthodox, and High Orthodox. After the presentation I asked the Cantor why he had not mentioned the Hasidim sect, and he replied, "Are you crazy?" He felt that their fundamentalism would only confuse the students. I was not surprised by his response.

When we arrived at the Holocaust Centre for a tour, a man in the lobby sent the students upstairs with one teacher while the other teacher and I took the elevator. We went into an office near the elevator and introduced ourselves. A gentleman who was to be the speaker was there, and I introduced myself to him and told him I was a survivor. When I told him why I was there and where we were from, the lady at the desk interrupted rudely, saying, "And you live in Bracebridge? What's a woman like you doing in Bracebridge?" I was dumbstruck at that woman's ignorance and insensitivity. She was implying that I shouldn't be living away from the synagogues and Jewish people in Toronto. The teacher, Bonnie Dart, put her arms around me and replied, "We are happy she lives there; we need her." On the trip home the conversation focused on that woman's attitude. The teachers were surprised at the kind of treatment I had received. Later one of the teachers told me that the students had felt let down by the visit.

This was the same sort of treatment I had received four years ago when I went there to register for a taping session. I explained to the woman that it would be easier for me to do the taping in the summer when I was not needed to babysit my grandchildren. When I told her where I lived, she asked what I was doing living in Bracebridge? I replied that my son and family lived nearby and it was a beautiful resort area. When I told her I felt I had a mission there she said that was okay. Then she asked if my son had married a Jewish girl. I was furious at her attitude and her lack of respect for me as a person capable of making my own decisions. At that point I got ready to leave and she handed me some forms that referred to Bergen-Belsen. I took the forms and left, telling myself that I would not be coming back. I wonder if the director of the Holocaust Centre is aware that some survivors are treated disrespectfully by some of the employees or volunteers at the Centre. People working at the Centre should know better than anyone how important it is to treat all people with compassion and sensitivity.

Recently a woman from the Steven Spielberg Foundation in California contacted me and interviewed me for their files. She asked me questions about my origins, and the ghetto I had been in. She asked me if the foundation could film the interview and if it would be all right to do it on the Sabbath. I replied that both would be all right. Then she asked if there were any other survivors living in Bracebridge. I said I didn't know. I was told it would be a few months before they could come to Bracebridge, and that they would call me. This happened in late winter during 1997 and I'm still waiting, but not holding my breath. Why was I never contacted again? If they have decided not to do the interview, then they should be polite enough to let me know that.

These experiences suggest to me that since I do not live in Toronto in the Sheppard and Bathurst area, or any other Jewish district, the story of my adjustment after the Holocaust is of no consequence. Should I conclude that my experiences as a survivor have been rejected because of my where I live? Am I not considered a descendent of Abraham or the Cannanites because I do not live in a Jewish district? Recently I spoke to a Cantor who agreed with me, saying that wherever there is air, there is a descendent of Abraham. Why do some Jews send these mixed messages? The message I received at the Holocaust Centre was not God's message that we are all equal . Others have tried to put me down, unsuccessfully, including my sister.

21.

THE DANES

The beliefs and traditions of a culture can make a crucial difference in how its members behave in times of crisis. Why did racism and bigotry develop in some cultures and not in others? Why did some of the Dutch and French people behave in such an anti-Semitic way while the Danes and Swedes protected and sheltered Jews from the Nazis? Likewise, Romania and Bulgaria are neighbors with the same racial origin, but while the Romanians felt the need to slaughter and annihilate Jews, the Bulgarians felt the need to protect them. In all of these countries there were people who risked their lives to save Jews and many died in the process.

When Hitler invaded Denmark in 1940, the Danish people said, " The Jews are our neighbours. We live together, work together, and play together. Do not touch our neighbours." Hitler promised to leave the Jews alone. In the summer of 1943 Hitler broke that promise and ordered the Gestapo to deport thousands of Jews to German concentration camps. The Danes discovered these plans and acted immediately, arranging for boats to smuggle 7200 Danish Jews to Sweden. The Swedish people

welcomed these refugees into their country, giving
them food and shelter, and looking after all their needs.
The Danish and Swedish people showed that they
were humane. Their moral and spiritual strength
demanded that they prevent the Gestapo from carrying
out their plans. When the Nazis insisted that Jews
wear a yellow star, the Danish king, Christian, wore
one in public too, sending a strong message to the
Danish people that he identified with and supported
all his people.

In some of the occupied countries nine out of
ten Jews were killed. In Denmark nine out of ten Jews
survived. The crucial difference was the behaviour
of ordinary citizens who considered the Jews to be
their brothers and sisters. The properties of Jewish
people who had escaped to Sweden were made secure
until the end of the war. Rude told me about a Jewish
couple who returned to their apartment in Copenhagen
after the war was over and found it clean and tidy.
They had left in a hurry and their Danish neighbours
had gone into the apartment and cleaned it up. The
churches hid the Torahs and Jewish businesses were
made secure. When the Jews got back to Denmark,
everything was returned to them. What made these
people so special? In the 17th Century Denmark
passed a law banning religious or racial discrimination.
Was this the beginning of the tradition of Danish racial
and religious equality? Can we build another
Denmark? The world needs a lot more people like
the Danes.

This was very different from what happened

in Hungary and Romania. Many Hungarians, including the police, collaborated with the Gestapo and the SS. The Hungarian and Romanian armies fought alongside the Nazi armies and many atrocities were committed within their borders. Jews were slaughtered in both countries, their property was confiscated or destroyed, and synagogues were demolished. Approximately 750,000 Jews from both countries were deported to the death camps with the help of the local police, the army and civilians during the war.

Anti-Semitism was strong in Hungary in the 1920s and 1930s and even stronger in Romania before the war began. My parents told us how in 1922 Jewish students were murdered on their college campuses and higher education and certain occupations were denied to Jews. In Szatmar, when I was 13 or 14, young children shouted *"Tetves Zsido"* (Lousy Jews) at Jews on the street. These kinds of actions surprised me when I was young, but as I got older I realized that this was mild compared to what was happening all over Europe and North America. These Hungarian children took what they were taught at home by their parents out onto the streets. Children breathe the air they live in, in Hungary as well as Denmark.

I don't know of many other countries that stood up and refused to allow the Jews to be taken away. In Bulgaria some farmers protested by threatening to lie down on the railroad tracks to stop the trains carrying Jews to concentration camps. Even the churches and their leaders got involved. Unfortunately Bulgarian Jews who were living in other countries were unprotected. However, we are eternally grateful for every life that was saved. Other countries rejected the Jews and wouldn't accept us before the war. How many Jews tried to come into Canada and the United States in 1938 and were turned away? Many of those Jews ended up back in Germany and were sent to the death camps.

22.

JACKIE

I became very vulnerable after Rude's death, without a partner to share my life. Like many widows, I was seen as a threat by some of the women with whom I socialized. During the first five years I made some mistakes, but I believe that mistakes are really learning experiences, and in my case that was certainly true. My mourning period may have been different from that of other widows, but I had lived for three years with the constant fear of death, unable to share my grief with others, except for my dear friend, Jackie.

In the years following Rude's death my life centered on my son Jan. We travelled to the East Coast and cottage country and to Expo '67 in Montreal. Jackie and I spent a lot of time together, sewing clothes for each other — dresses, shirts, suits and blouses. It was a most helpful pastime for me at that time. We shared a lot of joy and sadness, both hers and mine. Eventually she persuaded me to enroll in the dance class at the YWCA and a social club for singles. I was scared out of my wits but determined to give it a try. This was about three years after Rude's death, and I was insecure and vulnerable. Jackie walked behind me with a big stick, very determined that I return to the social life. I enjoyed the dancing and socializing, and this club became a wonderful learning experience for me and enabled me to meet new people.

One of the people I met was Professor Sid Wilson, who was a very positive influence in my life. In the beginning I was not able to be open with him or share details about my past life, but we became friends. He was an intelligent, gentle soul who was much older than we were and had taught English at the University of Toronto. When my friend Olive brought him to my house for a visit, he and I talked about the war. I told him a little about my past but did not go into much detail. He suggested I write a book about my childhood and the Holocaust and said that he would be most honored to help me.

It would have been a great opportunity, but I wasn't ready to deal with my past then. I had to keep that door closed because I could not deal with the pain. Later the same week I received a dozen red roses from him with the message "Beauty to a Beauty." I thanked him very much but I had a difficult time accepting a gift from a man. Sid told me to remember the importance of receiving as well as giving, reminding me that without a receiver there cannot be a giver. I will always remember his teaching. Perhaps he could have become the father figure I would like to have had as I grew up. He died in the mid-70s at age 85, but his spirit is still with me. This relationship was easy and uncomplicated compared to some of those that were to develop later.

I went to work doing marketing research when my son was 17, just a year before he finished high school, and I discovered what a sheltered life I had been living. My friend Jackie was doing the same job and she helped me with my writing. When she says, "I taught Eva how to write English," I always kid her, "That's why I still don't know how to write." Jackie spent a lot of hours training me for the business world. She and I worked together as partners, doing random sample surveys around Toronto about different issues and products. She would follow me home every day after our shift and help me correct the spelling in my reports. This required patience and sensitivity on her part, but she is a very caring person and the bond between us grew stronger.

After so many years of isolation this experience was enlightening for me. Meeting people from all walks of life and engaging people in conversation opened my mind and broadened my perspective on human behaviour. Jackie and I enjoyed working together and had a lot of fun. Our spiritual bond has enabled us to continue our friendship to this day. We have been friends for 42 years now and it has been a very satisfying relationship — give-and-take, caring and sharing — and we are both very capable of that. Jackie's like a sister to me.

Some of us have had more tragedies in our lives than others, but I don't sit around feeling sorry for myself because of what has happened to me in the past. Some of the decisions we make are very good and some of them are not so good. My father's decision not to escape to Israel in 1943 resulted in the deaths of six of eight members of my immediate family. My parents decided to deny me an education and the space to develop in my own way because of their religious fundamentalism. My sister initially decided to deny me the right to be myself and now denies even my existence and considers me dead. I have thought many times that had we not come to Canada, my husband would still be alive today. I had already suffered enough; why did I have to lose 87 members of my family, one of my babies, my beloved husband? However, in the end we can never know why things happen as they do; we must try to survive and carry on.

Today I can say that it was better to have loved and lost than never to have loved at all. I get on with my life, making the best of each day, and having a mission helps me.

Elsie, Jackie's 92-year-old mother, has also been my "mother" for the last 42 years. Years ago she gave me a placemat that said, "Live one day at a time and make it a masterpiece." I have always cherished that placemat and it's stuck on my fridge door for me (and my grandchildren) to see. I try to live and breathe what that placemat says. Someone said, "Yesterday is history, tomorrow is a mystery, this moment is a gift and that's why it's called the present." It certainly is a gift I cherish; I have learned to live one day at a time.

Jackie's three children —Jeff, Linda and Greg

— love me. Jackie was pregnant with my godson Greg when I met her. Although we are not related I have been their "Aunt Eva" since 1956. When I look at Linda today I can still see a little white-haired girl walking to my house to talk to her Aunt Eva and share stories. As she matured into her teens our stories became more sad than happy. When we visit each other now we still talk about the stories we shared so long ago. Jeffrey, the oldest boy, is married and has two boys and a girl who are now in their teens. Gregory is also married but has no children and I see him and his wife more often than I see Jeffery. These caring people are my extended family and I will be their Aunt Eva for the rest of our lives.

23.

WORKING

I started working again when I was 64 years old. I babysat at home 45 hours a week and also went out to work seven days a week. While my friend Jackie and I were at a local hotel for dinner one evening, Jack, the owner, introduced himself and talked to us. I mentioned that I was Jewish and he said, "My mother is Jewish and she's staying at the hotel. Wait here and I will get her." We had a very pleasant conversation and he offered me a job as a waitress at the hotel. When I explained that I might have trouble writing down the orders in English, he suggested that I work at weddings and banquets, where I wouldn't have to write things down. I accepted his offer, but he kept pushing me to wait on tables because it was a very busy summer and they were short of waitresses. Jack suggested that I take a menu home and study it so I would be more comfortable writing orders.

After the tourist traffic slowed I agreed to try waitressing. I had a lot of negative experiences with the kitchen cooks, especially the male employees. They made references to my poor writing ability and my age, saying that I was taking a job away from a younger person. They told me I would get more money from the government if I stayed home than I would make working there. I would often go home from work crying because of the verbal abuse by the men in the kitchen. I did not want to complain to my boss but one day it became evident to him what was happening. He grabbed the offender by the shirt collar and said, "If I ever hear you speak to this lady like that again I'll punch you out and you'll be gone from here."

The positive side of my working there five and a half years was the feedback from my customers and the many friends I made. My customers were not concerned with how well I wrote their orders or the fact that I was working at my age. Some of my customers would even phone ahead to see if I was working and would be able to serve them when they arrived. I have more positive than negative memories about my waitressing job. One couple I will always remember made reservations a year in advance for their 50th anniversary and specified that they wanted me to serve them dinner and then breakfast for their whole family, a party of sixteen. They appreciated my services and I received a personal gift from them.

Working as a waitress and babysitting weren't easy but I managed. Sometimes I even worked a double shift of 19 hours. I'd serve at a wedding reception, then go into the dining room and work behind the bar or wherever I was needed. I never felt that it was too much or that I couldn't do it. I had to work to make myself financially independent because

I didn't believe in being supported by the government or someone else. I had to do it myself and was quite capable of doing just that. After my son and his wife picked up the children at 4:30, I went to work until 10 p.m. I worked longer hours on Saturday and Sunday because I didn't have the children. Both my son, Jan, and his wife, Kim, are teachers and could look after their children on weekends and in the summers.

24.

MY GRANDCHILDREN

My garden is important to me and my grandchildren, for they will remember how Bubba shared the fruits of her garden — carrots, flowers, tomatoes and raspberries. These are the seeds I want to plant. We have to plant positive seeds and help them grow, even if some seeds don't take too well. We have to try to turn whatever is negative in life into positives from which other positives can grow.

We have to give children the space to breathe. We cannot say no to our children all the time. We have to sit down and talk about how we can change things and make them better. This is what life is all about. What we give to these young people is extremely important. I have been physically close to my grandchildren all of their lives, but they are not always going to live beside me and I'm not going to be here forever, (although I would like to try). However, I'm quite sure they will remember me. My greatest happiness is watching them grow and develop.

I felt compelled to write this memoir when my

grandchildren began to ask questions about my past. I want them to see how I lived and know what my life's journey was like so they can appreciate their lives and make the most of each day, living in peace and harmony, caring for mankind, loving each other. When I hear them, as children do in every family, bickering or saying, "Oh, I hate this," I say, "Don't use the word hate; hate is a very strong emotion. Maybe you could say, 'I don't like this.' It's okay not to like something; we can't like everything or everyone."

I am happy that my story is being told in this book and in my talks to students, churches, and other organizations, as it means that my message will not be forgotten. Speaking openly helps me balance my life and ignore the mixed messages I receive from some people. I am sure that Rudy, with his insight and sensitivity, will carry my message forward throughout his life. The bond that exists between my grandson and me will always be part of the tape he will be taking with him, because the tapes we make as children are extremely powerful and important in our lives. Children can only give back what was given to them by those closest to them.

When my son was a young boy, I was told many times that I was too lenient, not strict enough, giving him too much care or not enough. It's very difficult to be strict and discipline children, because it often depends on how we feel at that moment. Should we discipline strictly or should we be more understanding? Perhaps we're angry because we are disappointed in ourselves. When my father used cruel discipline, I wondered whether it was for my benefit or for his. Discipline used with anger can achieve a short-term gain, but a long-term gain is preferable. How can we get around that? We parents should think before we discipline rather than react immediately to what a child is doing. We should put ourselves in the child's shoes. Should we expect our children to be perfect when we know very well that we are not? Sometimes we want them to be more like someone else, but the grass is always greener on the other side of the fence. There are lots of weeds there, just as there are weeds in our yard. We have to cultivate and add lots of TLC if we want growth.

My son is a high school teacher now, and recently a woman asked me to tell my son how much she appreciated him keeping her son off the streets by getting him involved in sports. When I mentioned this to my son he remarked that he hadn't done much more for that boy than he does for other students. He already has a lot to do as a teacher and father of three children, but he spends his free time keeping the kids off the street by getting them involved in other activities. He is a basketball coach for elementary school children, and he helped start a rowing club in town. I have been told by some of his students that I should be proud of him because he is their best teacher. I'm very proud of how my son turned out.

When my son was a youngster I gave him the freedom to express himself and to develop spirituality.

I can see that he is passing on to his children some of the strengths I was able to give him. He's a caring person who likes to share his happiness with others and that's very satisfying to me. I know I have raised a son who is a loving, caring, human being and I couldn't ask more of myself. In order to reach that goal I realized I needed to separate the son from the man. Only that way could I see him as an individual human being and appreciate the many qualities he is blessed with. It means a great deal to me that he has the freedom to choose the direction of his life and that of his family.

We need to remember the importance of treating our children with respect and dignity, so that when they grow up, they're going to treat their peers with respect and dignity. We must not underestimate our children's ability to understand. What they have been taught as children will be what they take with them as adults. When we make a loaf of bread and don't put in enough yeast, it might rise a little bit, but if we put in just the right amount we get exactly the loaf we want. If we expect tomorrow's leaders to be people we can look up to, then we have to give them the right ingredients to make them responsible adults.

My grandchildren are developing their own personalities. They are all different and I love them all differently for the way they are. Who knows what they will be like when they're older? I'm sure they will have lots of good things to take into the world to help themselves and others.

When she was 13 Brenna interviewed me about

my childhood and my experiences during the Holocaust. She wrote quickly as I spoke and edited her notes later because her speech could only be five or six minutes long. She invited me to be present when she gave her speech along with a dozen grade-eight students who were participating in the contest. Brenna delivered her speech well, and it was a very emotional experience for all of us. I saw people crying. When she finished speaking she came over to where I was sitting, put her arms around me and we cried together. That moment of contact was indescribable. People were overwhelmed that a 13-year-old girl could have such strong feelings and was able to share them with us. Until then I would have not believed that Brenna was capable of such emotional depth. She has always been deep in my heart and soul, but that day she bore herself into my heart deeper than I could ever have imagined. She must have held those emotions in for a long time but that day they came out. Seeing my grandchildren choosing to show their feelings really helps me.

Brenna was my first grandchild and I was overwhelmed when she came along. I babysat her every day from the time she was 13 months old. She has always been a little on the shy side, not quite sure of herself at times. Maybe it's always that way with the first child. I just let her be herself and that has helped her. I know she will be less shy and more secure in herself as she matures. She certainly has proved to be very different than I thought she was. I underestimated her before, but now I see that she is capable of whatever she puts her mind to. We should never underestimate the ability of children.

Rudy was born next, and I started to babysit him when he was nine months old. When he was six, Rudy asked me how my mother had died and I told him I would tell him when he was older. In the fall, when he was seven, he came back to me and said, "Bubba, I am older now and I want you to tell me how your Mama died." I thought that if he was old enough to ask me such questions he deserved answers, even though my answers might be very traumatic to a seven-year-old boy. I told him how my mother went to the gas chamber along with her three little grandchildren. Of course, I couldn't tell him this story without being moved emotionally. He sat down beside me and said, "Bubba, I am sorry that you are so sad." Sometimes sharing pain is necessary to teach children how to deal with pain. Their feelings are very important. Rudy is very much like me when I was his age. I can see he has a lot of my genes. I first noticed how much he cared about others when he was five; he reminded me of myself at that age. He's always willing to help, always caring, asking, "How are you today, Bubba? Are you feeling okay? Did you have a good day?" That's Rudy. I know there are a lot of outside influences in his life and some of these will be negative. I have faith in his ability to sort things out and make positive choices in his life as he matures. I hope he will always have the same freedom his father was given.

A few years ago I was asked to speak to a

sociology class for three consecutive days on five different world issues, including the Holocaust. Rudy would visit me when he came home from school each day and ask how I'd made out at the high school. He wanted to know what I talked about each time, so I told him and shared the student responses with him. On the third day he said to me, "Bubba, you may not be able to teach them from books, but you can teach them from your heart." Those were powerful and insightful words to be coming from such a young person. He also encouraged me and hoped that I would receive more invitations to speak.

I have babysat my youngest grandchild, Alexandra Leah, from the time she was five-and-a-half months old, and she has the wonderful gift of always being able to make me laugh. She comes to see me every day, sometimes setting up a make-believe store in my den and trying to sell me assorted items. At other times she watches television with me, with her head on my lap and holding one of my hands. She came in from school one day and asked me what day is was. I told her it was Monday, and she said "Oh, that's why it smells so good in here." On Mondays I cook and bake bread to share with others. It's nice to know this will be part of her memory of me. When she was away on a family trip she sent me a postcard: *Dear Bubba, I am having a good time, but I miss you very much. I picked some seashells and I am going to give you one because you are so loving, sharing and caring. I love you.* I cried when I read it.

My grandchildren mean a lot to me because
of my past. Perhaps it is different than for other people
who have not experienced what I have and can't relate
to my need for a balanced life. Grandchildren are
lovely. A woman once said to me that the best thing
about grandchildren is that you have them for two
hours and then you send them home. Well, that's
one way of loving your grandchildren and enjoying
them, but I needed my grandchildren for more than
just a couple of hours. Another lady told me that she
didn't know anyone more unselfish than me, and I
said, "That's not quite true. I am selfish at certain
times. I want those children beside me because they
are my family and give me great joy.

I also want to give of myself to my
grandchildren." Perhaps in some way they have taken
the place of Mama's grandchildren. God works in
mysterious ways. My nieces were annihilated in such
a horrific way, but I have been able to know and
enjoy my adorable grandchildren and free to give
them something of myself. Lots of children are well
cared for in good daycare centres, but they are still
missing the family touch. I would not have been
happy if my son and his wife had put the
grandchildren in daycare centres. I know Jan and
Kim were very happy that I was available as a sitter
for my grandchildren for 12 years. I still have them
under my wing from time to time, but now that they
are older and go to school I don't need to babysit
them as often. Still, when the bus drops them off
Bubba is there to give them a little snack and see that

they're looked after. It was important to me that my grandchildren get to know me rather than a stranger. I'm sure it helps their parents too, knowing that it's not some stranger looking after their children.

25.

SPEAKING TO STUDENTS

Throughout my recent journey I have been grateful for the enthusiasm of both students and teachers, an indication that the upcoming generation is aware of the importance of spirituality and tolerance. These two elements will make it easier for them have faith in themselves, love all of mankind and accept their differences. If they love themselves they will be better able to deal with the negative experiences in their lives, just as I have had to deal with loss and deprivation in mine. If they don't love themselves they won't be able to love anybody else. Sometimes this brings out anger in people — they hate others because they're unable to love themselves.

When I speak to students I stress that I need them to help me to promote tolerance by making sure it is part of their everyday lives. I point out that mere tolerance is not enough; we must develop deep respect for each human being. Sometimes they may think that a little bit of bigotry or racism doesn't hurt anybody, so they do nothing and say nothing. But this is the same as condoning it. We are all citizens of this universe and the only way humanity can survive is if we share and care for each other. We cannot stand back and let racism grow. We must not allow intolerance. If we keep killing each other, what does that say about the kind of world we want?

Why do I spend the time talking to young people? I trust them and I have faith in them. My goal is to reach the younger generation because they will carry on my work. I think this generation has a better chance of standing up against an evil power — if they know what to watch for. None of us knows where or when an evil power will arise next, so we have to be on guard constantly. They must remember that racism is a very bad thing. It doesn't apply to just one group.

I have received over a thousand letters from students, and these show me that they want a better society and want to care for others. As the following excerpts show, they are hearing my message about the dangers of bigotry and intolerance and applying it to their own lives:

Dear Eva,   January 21, 2000

I honestly don't know how you could keep going but am I ever glad you did. You showed me that you have to keep going and never give up. You also showed me how important it is to be kind to others. It isn't good enough to keep from being mean to someone; you have to be nice to them too. I've also learned that you should try to get other people to do the same. ... You are teaching my generation how we must get along and respect each other in order to survive. Without respect for each other the world will not function.

Brittney Parlett (Monsignor Michael O'Leary Separate School)

Dear Eva,

Once again you have touched my heart with your story. This time I heard it in much more detail, which I found quite disturbing. You remain my hero. ... From the first time I heard you speak you changed my thoughts and views... You helped me to realize how precious life is and how we can use our lives to touch and teach others. I am not sure why I'm here or what my role is but you helped me to realize I'm here for a reason. I hope that someday I'll find out. Over the last three years you and my parents have been my role models... I look up to you and admire you more than you'll ever imagine. I know that those who lost their lives in this horrific event are looking down on you and admiring your strength and courage.

I love you and you will continue to be part of me for the rest of my life. I want you to remain in my life and I hope we have more opportunity to spend time with each other. Wherever I travel in this world I will always carry a part of you in me... You are a wonderful person who I love so much.

Lots of love,
Jennifer Dobie (Bracebridge & Muskoka Lakes SS)
November 3, 1999

Dear Eva,

When I heard you speak on Thursday in Mrs. Dart's World Issues class, I felt more love for someone I had just met than I have ever felt in my whole life. I do not want to say that I was racist in any way towards you, but I was a racist. I never really knew why and I had no reasons for my actions; it was just something that I felt inside of me. Today I stand strong, saying that I am not a racist person any longer. I believe in all the different types of people ... people are all the same on the inside, no matter what they act like or look like. I would like to thank you for making me realize this. If you had not come into our class and spoken it might have been a long time before I realized what I was doing wrong. Your words were so powerful ... your face was so understanding. I could have sat on those uncomfortable plastic chairs for the whole day and listened. Most of the time I am a loud and outspoken person. You helped me realize that you do not have to be loud for people to understand you. If they are kind people they will understand you for who you are, no matter what. To deal with the loss of and separation from ... your very own family must have been hard enough for you. Your ability to speak to a classroom full of teenagers about something in your life that was more tragic than anything that could happen to me is an ability I respect. I believe you are a role model for all the children, teenagers and adults you speak to. You have the ability to help people realize what the world is really about. I listened attentively throughout your presentation, but I have to tell you that when you spoke of all the death and hatred ... in those concentration camps I had to turn my head. I had to close off my ears to what you were saying because I had never heard anything as powerful or as moving as what you told us.

I would not say that I am sheltered from our world but I would not say that I know everything about what is going on either. I have never really been interested in learning what happened before our time and I have never really kept up on things that would hurt to hear. When countries go to war I have to say I will be the last to hear about it. This is because I have told myself that I do not want to hear about it. I am an emotional and very sensitive person; I do know right from wrong. What those people did to you and many others was inhuman; that is the only word I can think of for them... I'm sorry for tuning you out when you were speaking but I did it because I knew that I would not be able to handle the truth. I feel better that I know, but I did not want to know that those poor children died smelling their own flesh burning. I did not want to know that your mother, father, and family died before you could say that you loved them and I did not want to know that in our world there are people who can do such things to other people and feel no remorse.

As the tears streak down my face I can smile because I know that as I left that classroom I had the strongest feeling of hope and happiness I will ever have in my entire life. You gave me this hope and I will hold onto it as you did and are still doing today. ... I have never hugged a complete stranger and felt as much compassion as I did when I hugged you. Thank you for what you said to me and thank you for helping me. I will always remember what you told us, Eva, and I will never forget what you gave me.

Robyn McKee (Bracebridge & Muskoka Lakes SS)
September 16, 2000

EPILOGUE

Today, simple things make me happy — getting up at 6:30, sitting quietly with my coffee, looking out at the river, where I see trees, birds, water, boats, and people fishing. It's soothing to my soul to live in a country where we have so much freedom and I pray people will never take it for granted. I certainly don't, because I was deprived of so much at one time or another in my life.

I am very fortunate in many ways. I am now reasonably healthy, emotionally balanced and spiritually strong, able to cope with and survive whatever comes my way. Being able to share my time and talents (especially cooking and sewing) with others makes me happy and content. My mission to help young people fight intolerance and bigotry by speaking about my life has given me new strength and purpose.

I appreciate having a garden and being free to grow whatever I like. My garden supplies food for my family and nourishes my soul. I have planted some miniature rose bushes in memory of my five nieces. I look after these roses, talk to them and give them the tender love and care I would have given my nieces. They will never be forgotten.

At 7:30 Alexandra comes to me with hugs and kisses before she goes to school. As Brenna walks to the school bus she looks to see if I'm at the window and gives me a wave. Fifteen minutes later Rudy arrives, but if he's late he knocks on my kitchen window as he goes by.

I am truly blessed.

Paintings by Laura Thompson (Twin Lakes Secondary School, Orillia)

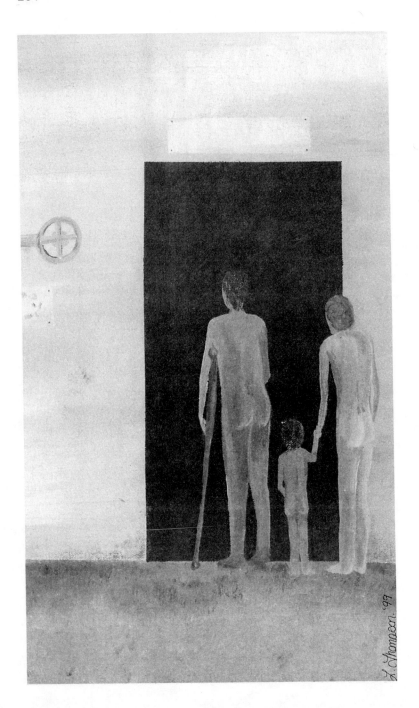

Ordering Information

To order additional copies of this book

By Mail:

Eva Olsson

RR 4

Bracebridge Ontario

P1L 1X2

By Phone:

(705) 645-2120   (local)

1-888-477-2224   (toll-free)

Cost: $19.95 plus $5.00 (Canadian) shipping and handling per book, payable to "Eva Olsson." Cheque or money order only, please.